⸺•| *THE* |•⸺
EXECUTIVE
INTERVIEW

·| *THE* |·
EXECUTIVE
INTERVIEW

MARIAN FAUX

ST. MARTIN'S PRESS
NEW YORK

Editor: Barbara Anderson
Production Editor: Mitchell Nauffts
Copy Editor: Ina Shapiro

Library of Congress Cataloging in Publication Data
Faux, Marian.
   The executive interview.
   1. Employment interviewing.   2. Communication
in management.   I. Title.
HF5549.5.I6F38   1985   650.1'4'024658   85–10058
ISBN 0-312-27428-9

First Edition

10 9 8 7 6 5 4 3 2 1

Contents

Introduction

I decided to write this book when I realized that while there were books on various aspects of executive job-hunting, such as how to work with a headhunter, how to write a resume, even how to emanate power, there were no books about how to get through an executive job interview. I found this particularly odd because most experts believe the interview is the single toughest aspect of getting a job. Some experts say the interview is the *only* thing that matters. They note that a job candidate can have great contacts—including sponsorship by a top headhunter—an exemplary track record, and an excellent resume, and that none of this will matter if he or she doesn't pass the interview with flying colors.

What makes the executive interview so difficult? For one thing, it is based almost entirely on chemistry. At the lower levels of management, people are hired primarily because they have a special skill or area of expertise. At the executive level, where leadership is the commodity that's being bought and sold, it is a candidate's ability to get along with and manage others that counts. And one of the most important times to show off this ability is during an interview. Unfortunately, too few executives understand or appreciate the extent to which chemistry determines the outcome of an executive interview. Of those executives who do understand its role, most still aren't sure how to create the chemistry that will ensure a successful executive interview. This book will describe various ways to do just that.

The executive interview is also difficult because it is such a role reversal of the executive candidate's usual power relationships. In an interview, executives, who are used to wielding power over others, find themselves in a situation in which someone wields total power over them. The situation is fraught with danger.

Finally, the executive interview poses problems for executive job candidates because it is the one aspect of job hunting that cannot be delegated. An executive can hire a placement specialist to find contacts for him; he can hire someone to write his resume; he can hire an image specialist to show him how to dress and act; but he can never hire someone to take his place at a job interview. This the executive must do alone simply to survive, and he must do it well to succeed.

I hope that *The Executive Interview* will help both seasoned executive job hunters and those who aspire to the executive ranks to master the interview process.

I would also like to say a few words about the way in which this book was written.

Although I have attempted to pair female and male pronouns as much as possible, to avoid awkwardness and for the sake of brevity I have occasionally opted for the exclusive use of "he" and "him." I hope that the reader will forgive this bow to editorial taste and will understand that no exclusion was intended.

I am indebted to many people who shared their expertise and thus helped me write this book. I talked, on and off the record, with more than a dozen headhunters, and interviewed outplacement specialists, consultants, and placement counselors.

Of the experts who particularly helped me, in the sense of not only giving me information but also shaping my ideas, I would be remiss if I didn't mention Robert Hecht of Lee-Hecht & Associates; John Foster of Boyden Associates; Alfonso Duarte, Jr., of Korn/Ferry International; William Byham, president of Development Dimensions International; and Kathryn Stechert, a writer whose expertise is women and work.

I am also grateful to the dozens of job candidates who so generously shared their experiences and anecdotes with me.

Finally, I would like to thank Barbara Anderson for her keen editorial eye and her role in shaping this manuscript.

—MARIAN FAUX
New York City

·| THE |·
EXECUTIVE
INTERVIEW

· | *ONE* | ·

The Executive Interview

The executive interview is a trial by fire that you, if you are one or aspire to be an executive, must go through not once but several times during your career. It is the single most important hurdle you must clear to get the job you want. Everything else about job hunting is peripheral to the interview. You can send out a fascinating and articulate resume, write a stunningly impressive cover letter, and even be related to the chairman of the board, but unless you can present yourself and your qualifications effectively during the interview, chances are you won't land the job of your dreams.

Furthermore, even if something about you is not quite right for the job—let's say your qualifications aren't exactly what the company is seeking, for example—if you do well during an interview, there is a good chance you will still get the job. Or if you are one of three final candidates, and you all have approximately the same experience and education, then the way you perform during an interview may be the deciding factor. This is because chemistry is often a critical factor in determining whether or not you will get a job.

CHEMISTRY COUNTS MORE THAN YOU CAN IMAGINE

An interview is your only opportunity to find out if the chemistry is right. Because prospective employers have been burned enough times by employees, they have finally begun to incorporate some standards and procedures into the hiring process. It's still a well-known fact, however, that interviewers don't necessarily pick the "best," i.e., the most outstanding or the most qualified, candidate for a job. They pick the person with whom they have the best chemistry.

Let's face it. The average executive spends more hours a week, a month, year in and year out, with his colleagues than he or she spends with family members. You simply have to be congenial. Even more important, you have to share the same outlook about the really important management issues that determine how a company is run. Because of this, even the toughest, most critical, and most independent employer still tries to hire someone who looks like a team player, who will be pleasant to work with, and who can get along with other people. This is ultimately what being a manager is all about, and executives are really just top-of-the-line managers. John D. Rockefeller, Jr., understood the value of team players when he said, "The ability to deal with people is as purchasable a commodity as sugar or coffee. And I pay more for that ability than for any other under the sun."

If you can go into a job interview and show that the chemistry is right between you and the person across the desk, you will have done a lot to convince him or her that the chemistry will also be right between you and everyone else on the team. You're on the right track to getting the job.

WHY EXECUTIVES DON'T INTERVIEW WELL

Despite the importance of chemistry, it's not unusual for an executive to interview poorly. Some job candidates fail interview after interview, while others seem to lose out only on the big ones. Many executives are aware that they don't interview well, but still don't know what to do to improve their interviewing skills—or even if that's the problem. Most executives are polished enough, at least on the surface, to carry off an interview. Most are qualified for the jobs for which they interview. Most project the right image in their dress, their speech, even in their body posture. Their handshakes are appropriately firm. Most pass the social tests.

So what goes wrong? The reason so many executives don't interview well has nothing to do with these things, although they all are important to successful interviewing. The real problem lies in the fact that executives have to interview at all. The mere act of interviewing for a job goes against the grain of most managers' personalities.

Interviewing involves a major role reversal for most executives. This is the single most important reason that executives don't interview well. An executive executes, and, for most managers, this means questioning people, evaluating them, analyzing them, and making decisions about the quality of their future work—the very same considerations that occur during an interview. It shouldn't be surprising, then, that a high-powered executive may turn in a disappointing performance when the tables are turned, that is, when the manager is the one being questioned, evaluated, analyzed, and made the object of an important decision. Interviewing, more than any other part of job hunting, reverses the power relationship that most executives are used to dealing with on a day-to-day basis.

UNDERSTANDING THE INTERVIEW PROCESS

The executive interview can be viewed in many ways. It is:

* an exchange of ideas
* a conversation
* a sales pitch
* a performance
* an act of communication

Above all else, an interview is an act of communication. Your ability to communicate your experience and qualifications to the interviewer, and his ability to communicate the responsibilities, functions, and power of the position to you, are the two most important things that occur during an interview.

Executives are hired for their communication skills, so you absolutely must be able to project yourself as a good communicator during an interview.

An interview is not an intellectual exercise. Too often, job candidates confuse communicating with showing off. The skills required to do a managerial job are, for the most part, applied rather than intellectual. The person who goes into an executive interview intent on showing off his intellect, as opposed to his intelligence, is likely to appear condescending and overbearing.

An interview is an exercise in power. An interview is a rare occasion when you are free to operate on a peer level with the interviewer, who will almost always be your boss once you are hired. You will never have more negotiating power on a job than you will have going into it—that is, during the interviewing process. You negotiate your biggest raises and most meaningful perks when you are in the process of interviewing for a job, or, as one executive who has done a lot of hiring over the years put it: "You get your biggest raises by changing jobs. Once someone has hired you, he will never again have the same incentive to please you that he does on the day when you sit across the desk from him in an interview and he knows that you are the person he really wants to fill this job." It's imperative, then, that you understand how the balance of power works during an executive interview.

THE MATING DANCE: WHAT INTERVIEWS ARE ALL ABOUT

Understanding the balance of power is the most important key to a successful executive interview. In non-executive interviews, the prospective employer holds most of the power, and the interviewee is clearly a subordinate.

In an executive interview, the power is evenly distributed. Both the candidate and the interviewer bring an equal amount of power to the interview.

Unfortunately, this doesn't always result in the control shifting back and forth the way it should for an interview to be successful. The interviewer may dominate the interview, or, in certain circumstances unique to an executive interview, the candidate may dominate the interview.

When one person dominates an interview, the interview is rarely successful. Neither party accomplishes enough to get an accurate assessment of the other person. Because of this, some experts advise deliberately splitting the control. They say the interviewer should maintain control during the first half of the interview, and the candidate should take it during the second half. Experts argue that the interviewer needs the first half of the interview to describe the functions and responsibilities of the job, and the interviewee needs the second half, once he or she knows what the job is, to ask questions and describe the ways that his or her qualifications mesh with the job requirements. But as natural as this method of splitting control seems, it is all wrong for an executive interview. It is wrong because it misses what an interview is really all about.

Interviews are small-scale exercises in power that reflect the large-scale exercises in power that occur in daily office life. Because of this, an artificial situation is created when control is arbitrarily split between the two parties during the first and second halves of an interview.

A much more natural situation is to let the balance of power swing back and forth often throughout an interview, much as it does in daily office life. This gives both the interviewer and the candidate a more realistic picture of each other. Specifically, it gives each of them an accurate look at how the other spars for power. The only way, then, that the power relationship can operate successfully during an executive interview is for the control to become dynamic, a continuous exchange throughout the interview.

There are several ways to make this happen. If an interviewer is skilled, he or she will make it happen. Sometimes both the interviewer and the candidate have enough skill to make this happen. Sometimes, it happens by accident. More often than not, it doesn't happen at all. Many interviewers are not only unskilled but also downright inept at interviewing. In these all-too-common situations, the candidate must take control to ensure that the power bounces back and forth as it should. This book is devoted to showing you how to create situations in which the balance of power continuously shifts back and forth throughout an interview.

When this dynamic occurs during an interview, it is easy for both parties to see what they want and what they are getting. The interview then becomes a kind of mating dance. Both parties court each other to the point where consummation is urgently desired. The interviewer feels that the job candidate is the best person to fill the job and subsequently mounts a rigorous campaign to interest the candidate in the job. The candidate becomes confident that this is the right job for him at this stage of his career and tries equally hard to convince the interviewer of this. Everything about the job, including how well-suited the candidate is to this particular job, is communicated during such an interview.

When this process goes well, a job candidate—YOU—is hired into a job with far more clout and status than he or she might otherwise be accorded. This is why it is of tantamount importance that you understand how to interview well—that you know how to dance to the unique music of an executive interview.

TWO

What's In, What's Out— Styles and Trends in Executive Interviewing

No smart executive can afford to go into an interview without knowing what to expect—what kinds of interviews are popular today, what paces he or she will be put through, what is entailed in the interview process itself. And although this obviously varies from company to company, there are fads in interviewing as there are in anything else. Stress was in a few years ago; now it's so out that an executive should think twice about going to work for any interviewer who subjects him to the kind of stress games that were popular in the recent past. There are also styles and trends in interviewing, and these change every few years.

HUMAN RESOURCES DEPARTMENTS ARE RED-HOT

The major trend in interviewing in the past ten years is the increased amount of power that human resources departments wield. For years, personnel interviews were reserved for the clerical jobs and for some low-management positions. Executives were interviewed by other executives, and one of the perks of having achieved a certain amount of status was that no one would dream of subjecting you to the personnel department. Today, though, even at the top levels of hiring—CEOs and division managers—the interviewing process often begins with the personnel department, better known these days as human resources or organization development. And make no mistake about it, the executives who run these departments have clout. One executive recruiter, speaking rather wistfully of the days when he, too, bypassed personnel to work directly with CEOs and boards of directors, noted, "Where human resources are involved in the hiring process, they pass very important judgments."

THE HUMAN RESOURCES INTERVIEW

Now that human resources have begun to flex some real muscle, you need to know what to expect so that you're prepared for the initial interview.

Always try to find out whether you're up against a strong human resources department before you go into an interview. If you are, the interview will probably be conducted by a high-ranking executive—perhaps even by the top person in the human resources department—and he or she will probably have direct access to the CEO or possibly even the board of directors, depending upon the level of the search. There are no industry guidelines about who has a strong human resources department and who doesn't; you have to use your contacts to find out what the situation is in each individual case. One executive recruiter noted: "RCA, for example, is well known as a strong human resources company. IBM is strong, too. In banking, human resources departments are of about average strength. The older, more established industrial companies tend to have the best human resources departments. Some of the high-tech companies have good human resources departments, but a lot don't have any. Many of the smaller firms rely on professional search firms, but the bigger firms, such as IBM, DEC, or Data General, have their own data banks on individuals, and they often do all their own searches except at the very top levels, as, for example, when they're looking for a CEO, or when they need an unusual amount of confidentiality. The fact that so many companies maintain their own data banks also gives the human resources departments extra strength these days."

Most recruiters interviewed for this book cited IBM, DEC, RCA, and Data General as companies having strong human resources departments, but they are by no means the only companies that are strong in this area. You'll need to check up on each company before you go into the interview.

When you must go through a human resources interview, make the most of it. Often, the human resources department interviewer can supply you with important background information that you can use during your interview with the line executive. The human resources executive can answer questions about the company's culture, history, philosophy, and general background. Human resources people make it their business to know about these things, and although you should realize you will be getting the party line, it's still useful information.

Don't count on the human resources interviewer for much more than background information. He or she is not the person to rely on for accurate information about the job. Job functions and responsibilities are best discussed with the line executive. During the human resources interview, concentrate on making a good first impression so you'll be passed on to the executive who can fill you in on the job—and give it to you.

Beware of the traps that can be set for you in human resources. Many companies have begun to realize the true potential of the human resources department to evaluate personalities and now use these departments to test job candidates, sometimes in rather unorthodox ways. A recruiter described the situation at one established high-tech company this way: "The personnel person is even a nonpersonnel person, and a very young person, and a female person. A man who did not really understand what was going on could think he was being interviewed by a clerk. If he didn't read this situation right, he could be dead in two minutes."

One Fortune 500 company leaves a male candidate alone in a room with an attractive woman, who chats with him somewhat seductively and offers him coffee. Unbeknownst to the candidate is the fact that he is being videotaped, and that his reactions to the woman and the situation she presents will be "interpreted" later on by those who interview him more officially.

In another instance, a job candidate meets first with the human resources person and then is accompanied by that person on the round of interviews that have been scheduled for him. The person sits in on all the interviews primarily to verify that the candidate is telling each line executive the same things about his skills and experience.

THE FADS OF INTERVIEWING

Speaking of the fads that beset business from time to time, one management consultant said, "About every five years, management looks for a new hoola hoop. Five years ago, stress was the hot topic. The new hoola hoops are psychological assessment, job simulation, and interview by committee."

Psychological Testing:
An Old Hoola Hoop Arises Again

Largely under the auspices of the human resources departments, companies have once again begun to assess executive job candidates before hiring them. Sometimes, the tests are simply what human resources people call "pencil and paper tests"; at other times, a job candidate under serious consideration for a high-ranking managerial position is asked to spend an entire day being assessed by an outside psychologist. It's interesting that while these tests have fallen off for low management and clerical workers, they have assumed new importance in the top and middle ranks of management.

There is not much you can do to avoid psychological testing if you want a job. You're suspect the minute you refuse—even on logical grounds—to take a test, and you probably won't be considered further for the position.

Job Simulation: The Newest Hoola Hoop

So many companies have been burned so many times by hiring the wrong person that it's not surprising that yet another technique—that of job simulation—has also gained popularity.

In job simulation a candidate is asked to perform some part of the job he would be expected to handle if he or she were hired. This can be anything from writing a report to making a speech. For example, RCA occasionally asks job candidates to make a 1½- to 2-hour oral presentation centered around the functions of the job. Requesting such a presentation is often enough to make some candidates withdraw from the competition.

The Panel Interview

The panel interview, more descriptively known as interview by committee, is the last of the hoola hoops. As stress interviews declined in popularity, panel interviews became more widely used, even though most executive recruiters say panel interviews are really stress interviews and try to discourage them whenever possible. One company even does an unusual panel interview by bringing in the four or five final job candidates and interviewing them at the same time. According to someone who sat in on these interviews, "They might as well be putting the job candidates up against a firing squad. It's the most ridiculous interviewing technique I've ever heard of in my life."

Al Duarte, a vice-president and executive recruiter at Korn/Ferry International, compared a panel interview to meeting your future parents-in-law: "You've got to meet them both at once because that's the way these things are done." He advises giving yourself a pep talk to build up your self-confidence and doing everything you can to maintain it during the interview. Duarte added that panel interviews have to be very well planned to work at all, and that they're very stressful for job candidates, a view shared by all recruiters.

Panel interviews are conducted on several levels. The most frequent is when the job candidate is interviewed by peers. One experienced job hunter reported on her ordeal by committee: "It was arranged by a woman who believed that my prospective colleagues should be in on the interview with me. I didn't find it that bad. They didn't know what to do, so I had to do something. They weren't structuring the interview and were talking about the weather, so I picked up the ball and ran with it. I said to them, 'I'm really interested in hearing more about how you work, and maybe you could tell me more about it.' I asked questions about job functions. They should have done that to me. As they described their work, they asked me a couple of questions. It was easy, though, because once you know what someone does, you can relate anecdotes and stories that show you're with them, that you do the same thing or can do the same thing they do. As I went along with the interview, I also assessed which were the people I had the best personal rapport with and which were the ones I'd better give more eye contact to."

A more treacherous panel interview is one conducted by people who will be your superiors, and, of course, the very toughest interview of all is when you meet with the board of directors— an event that occurs almost exclusively when you are being considered for a CEO position.

Ned Klumpf, a management consultant and career counselor who has advised many executives on how to handle this situation, has this to say about being interviewed by a group of your potential superiors: "It's very difficult to handle being interviewed by any kind of committee. You sit there and wait for questions to be fired at you and you answer them. And if you're smart, you stick to accountability, authority, and responsibility. You use a lot of managerial terms. You try to keep it as objective as possible.

"You see, what really happens in a panel interview is that people think they're being objective, and on the surface these interviews do look objective, but in reality, a panel interview just opens the door for everyone to display his or her idiosyncratic preferences. After the interview, the managers get together, and then the power playing really starts. That's when objectivity goes down the drain. It's a very subjective interview. One person can say, 'I didn't like the way he looked at us.' Another can say, 'She really had a limp handshake.' There's too much room for that kind of posturing. None of it is objective."

A panel interview with the members of the board may be less subjective and petty than one among peers or superiors simply because so much more is at stake, but it usually consists of a very tough grilling. Passive people fade fast in these interviews. You either know the right answers or you don't. You either give the appearance of being a company player or you don't. If you don't look like a member of the team, though, nine times out of ten, you won't even have made it to the boardroom for the interview, if that's any consolation.

How to Get Through a Panel Interview

Some things will help to ensure your success during an interview by committee.

- **Be sure your eye contact is very good.** In particular, when you answer a question, look directly at the person who asked it.
- **Play to the person in power only after you are sure who this is.** Even then, be careful about focusing too much attention on one person. The relationships among the interviewers, their titles not withstanding, are probably too subtle to be understood in such a short time.
- **If someone is hostile to you, treat him or her with special respect.** Ask that person questions to force him or her to interact with you on a one-to-one basis.
- **Be prepared to take control if no one else does.** Almost without exception the only time you will have to do this is when you are with peers. You probably can't—and certainly shouldn't—take control from a committee of your superiors or from the board of directors.

Apart from these hoola hoops, you're also liable to encounter some other interviewing techniques and trends that are currently popular.

DIRECTED VERSUS NONDIRECTED INTERVIEWS

As more and more executives have brushed up on their interviewing techniques, nondirected interviews have gained in popularity. Frankly a nondirected interview is something that is best conducted by a trained psychologist who knows what he is doing and why. In the world of business, this is rarely the case, and line executives occasionally conduct this kind of interview.

In a nondirected interview, the interviewer deliberately remains passive and unusually quiet. In other words, he gives the job candidate lots of room to talk himself into a bad situation. In the hands of a trained human resources person, this interviewing technique can work to test how aggressive and energetic you are, but in the hands of a nontrained line executive, it can make for a lot of awkward silences.

If you are sure you are in a nondirected interview (the silences will be a dead giveaway), answer all the questions that are put to you. If you can do it naturally, ask a question that points the interview in a new direction or takes it further based on the most recent question. For example, if you were asked to describe what in your experience makes you qualified for this position (nondirected interviewers tend to ask broad questions like this), you should answer the question, and then say, "Is there anything else about my experience that I can tell you, any special area you would like to hear more about?"

At some point, you may have to live with the silence. Just answer the question and then sit quietly until the next question is asked. This is when you must resist the urge to continue talking or say whatever comes into your mind. The silences you hear during an important interview are among the most deafening in the world, but they are also intended to egg you into saying something you shouldn't say. Resist the urge at all costs.

Fortunately, most executives are too action-oriented to conduct this kind of interview, so you won't encounter many of these from line executives. Human resources people are more likely to use some nondirected techniques in an interview, but are usually so subtle that you won't feel uncomfortable.

A directed interview is just the opposite of a nondirected interview. The interviewer usually assumes control, asks most of the questions (especially early on during the interview), and generally takes the lead. You do need to recognize the difference between a directed interview conducted by a skilled interviewer and one conducted by a domineering or dominant personality. If the interviewer is skilled, he or she will get around to letting you have your say. You will get a chance to ask your questions. If he or she isn't skilled, you may have to assume some control in order to ask the questions you need to have answered.

Give the interviewer some time before you shift the power balance. Out of nervousness, some interviewers have to get out their spiel either about themselves or the company before they can sit back and share the platform with you. Always wait to see what kind of interview you're in before you leap.

THE INFORMAL INTERVIEW

The most subtle interview is the informal interview. It's so subtle that you may not even know you've been interviewed until you learn that you didn't get the job.

The informal interview usually occurs during a social occasion. It may be a golf game, an afternoon on someone's yacht, drinks at a club, or, most commonly, over a business lunch.

Usually your only clue that you are being sounded out for a job is that the person who seeks out your company has the power to hire you. You may not know there is a job opening; the job may not even be discussed directly during your social encounter. But you will be asked about how happy you are in your present job, your management style, and your ambitions.

You can't acknowledge that this is an interview, either. You must express your views as if the two of you were peers engaged in a casual conversation. For example, if the interviewer says, "I don't think direct work experience is all that important in hiring a manager. What I look for is someone who is congenial—a good people handler," your response should be something like this: "I agree. All the technical training in the world won't guarantee that someone will get along with others and manage them well. That's important to me, too." In this way, you can progress to the point where you both know whether or not you have similar management styles and whether you would be compatible working together.

The informal interview may seem casual, but in reality it is a chance to assess much more about you than might be observed during a more traditional interview: Do you drink a lot? Do you know how to handle a fish fork? How affable are you? How well do you handle social situations? During a structured interview, any job candidate knows enough to be on his or her best behavior, but if you don't even realize you're being interviewed, you're much more likely to let down your guard. Your best defense against this kind of interview is to recognize that you are, in fact, being interviewed for a job and to conduct yourself accordingly. Be careful, though, not to stiffen up and turn an informal interview into a formal one.

THE RECRUITER-GENERATED INTERVIEW

Although executive recruiters will be discussed in greater detail later, the recruiter-generated interview is worth mentioning here because it represents such a strong trend. The number of job placements by executive recruiters has grown in recent years to the point where some companies conduct job searches only through search firms. Even companies with strong human resources departments use search firms for their top searches and in situations when confidentiality is important.

One big difference exists between going into an interview when a recruiter is presenting you and going into one on your own: **You have more power when you are being presented by a recruiter.** According to Al Duarte, "When you're being recruited, you go in on a one-on-one basis. You may not even want the job at that point; you have to be sold on it. You've got more power when you're coming through a recruiter. This interview is more of a fact-finding exercise on both sides."

It is still possible, with all the power you wield, to fail this kind of interview. The way most people do this is by throwing their weight around too much. For example, even with a recruiter-generated interview, many job candidates still start with the human resources department. And as Robert M. Hecht of Lee-Hecht & Associates, a human resources consulting firm, noted, this is where many executives make their biggest mistake: "Senior-level people, without realizing it, send nonverbal messages to interviewers who may not be able to offer them a job because they're not at a high enough level. They don't think these people are very important, or they don't realize they can stop them from being hired even if they can't hire them. Even though the job candidate is saying the right words, he sends nonverbal messages that often belie the content of the words.

"What do I mean by nonverbal messages? You get a $100,000-a-year senior executive who is being interviewed by a $30,000-a-year personnel worker, and the executive leans back in his chair, puts his hands behind his head, and talks down his nose as if to say, 'Here, young man or young lady, I'll tell you what you need to know,' but the message is that the junior person doesn't really understand the situation or that the executive is doing him or her a favor by responding to the questions. Often, these executives display intimidating behaviors that they use on the job but that at the moment don't fit the role they are playing of a candidate who is trying to sell himself, however subtly."

A similar way to fail this interview, or any interview for that matter, is to be rude or inattentive to the little people who surround the Big Boss. Reported the head of one human resources department at a major manufacturing company, "I get feedback about a candidate from my secretary. I ask her how she was treated or what her impressions were. I ask if the person was conversational with her, especially if the candidate had to wait for me outside the office for a few minutes."

This man offered a good general guideline for anyone when he said, "The assumption that an interviewee ought to make is that anybody he or she talks to can influence the hiring decision."

THE INFORMATION INTERVIEW

The last trend in executive interviewing—the information interview—has unfortunately fallen on hard times, partly because of its overuse by networkers.

The information interview, usually generated by the job candidate, is set up not to ask for a job but merely to gather information about one. For example, you may want to learn about the opportunities in a new field, and so you call someone you know who works in that field and ask him or her to spend some time discussing this with you.

The information interview works best when someone has a tie or relationship, however remote, to you. Millie McCoy of

Gould & McCoy, an executive search firm, commented: "I understand that the information-gathering interview has been heavily abused, but it still can be used if you've got a friend. I know so many people who do it very well, by using their school ties. You went to Harvard Business School with Joe Smith at such-and-such a bank, so you call him up and ask him if he'll just talk to you." Most of the time, Joe Smith is happy to talk to you.

Information interviews work because people feel powerful when they can help other people. People like to be helpful when they can, and they may even feel that they are paying off an old debt to someone who helped them find a job. An information interview can also backfire, as on those occasions when you find yourself sitting in some very busy executive's office. He made the appointment three weeks ago, feels honor-bound to keep it, but really doesn't have the time to sit down and talk with you. These interviews are best ended as quickly as possible, and there's nothing wrong with your suggesting that you've come at the wrong time and could perhaps call to set another date.

One veteran job hunter who spent over a year unemployed while he changed from publishing to public relations had this to say about information interviews: "The whole networking concept, which has been overused, really works. I would sometimes be sitting across a desk from somebody who was three or four or even five generations removed from how it all started. A friend would give me the name of somebody, and the somebody would give me another name. Some people were helpful and cared, and others just wanted me out of their offices. But there were a number of situations where I would have an information interview with someone, and a month or two later, the person would call and say, hey, I heard about something for you."

One very important thing to keep in mind about informa-

tion interviews is this: **Underneath every information interview is a person who wants a job.** That person is you. This means you should approach this interview as seriously as any other. Prepare just as hard for it as for any other interview; prepare especially hard, in fact, because you don't want to waste the time of someone who is making time to help you.

Finally, don't abuse an information interview. Never set one up under false pretenses, either by pretending to have a tie where you haven't or by blatantly pushing for a job when you have said your only purpose is to gather information.

WHAT'S OUT

In a word, what's out is s-t-r-e-s-s. Stress interviewing techniques, which ranged from the sublime to the silly (and frankly, most hovered around the silly), are no longer used. At least, obvious stress is out, and the only kind of stress that is acceptable is what experts like to call "fair stress"—throwing the occasional tough question at a job candidate, deliberately trying to rile the candidate a little, or requesting that the candidate perform some job simulation before an audience.

Definitely out are such tricks as handing a job candidate an object and asking him or her to sell it, asking him or her to take a phone call that is supposedly from a client but is actually from a colleague in the next room, offering a cigarette in a room where there is no ash tray, asking someone to sit down when there is no chair nearby, or simultaneous drilling by three or four executives. Even interrogation is out, although there are some tough bosses whose personal style is and always will be inquisitional in tone.

Robert Hecht noted the overall ineffectiveness of stress techniques, saying, "Even when people use trap questions or stress techniques, they generally don't work. They were long ago demonstrated to be of no value. The interview itself is stressful enough because the candidate has a job at stake, as well as a livelihood and self-esteem."

During World War II, the Office of Strategic Services conducted elaborate studies that confirmed that stress tests are ineffective. They are particularly ineffective in a business setting, since the typical person doesn't encounter a lot of high-level, unhealthy stress at work. Stress tests don't work because they can't create a lifelike situation, and because they generate a false response from the person being tested. People subjected to stress tests don't get their adrenaline flowing and rise to the occasion; they close up and feel defensive and guarded.

Occasionally, a company works out a fair stress test. One such company is Life Science Division of Whittaker Corporation, which provides hospital and health services to Saudi Arabia. They spend $10,000 to hire each employee, and employees sign an 18-month contract, so a mistake can be costly for everyone involved. They typically conduct three interviews, and one of these is a negative stress interview in which the interviewer attempts to tell the job candidate why he or she doesn't want the job. The last interview is supposedly with a person who will brief the job candidate on the culture and lifestyle in Saudi Arabia, but who is, in reality, one final interviewer. Many job candidates let down their guard and confess to fears that disqualify them for the job at this stage. Although the candidate is unaware of the degree of manipulation to which he or she is being subjected during this company's interview process, this is that rare stress interview that works in everyone's best interests.

Never Expect Form to Follow Function

In conclusion, although you're a step ahead of the competition if you know about the different kinds of interviews and how to handle them, never forget that each interview is unique. A company could set up the most stringent guidelines in the world for its executives to use in hiring, but as long as human beings are involved, interviews will remain highly personal in content and often intuitive in conduct.

·| *THREE* |·
How to Get an Executive Interview

When an interview goes well, those involved can virtually hear the clicks as the two people dance around one another, communicate with one another, find the areas where they match, investigate the areas where they do not match, and decide that these can still be strengths for each person. An interview that clicks doesn't happen every day— and it never happens entirely by accident. *You* must make it happen. Getting the right kind of executive interview is something you must know how to do. The first step in getting the right kind of executive job is finding the right interviewer.

HOW TO PINPOINT THE RIGHT INTERVIEWER

As a rule, you need to be interviewed by the person to whom you will report if you take the job. It may be the CEO, the chairman of the board, a division manager, or a line manager.

You can always start lower down the ladder of authority with a contact you have been given, with the human resources department,* for example, but this will lengthen the process.

---

* You may have no choice but to start with the human resources department, even for a very high position. These interviews were discussed in Chapter 2.

Sometimes the interview will result in a dead-end. It won't go anywhere, and you won't be recommended or passed on to the person who has the power to hire you. Especially with human resources people, the interviewer may not know there is an opening or may not realize that someone is thinking about creating an opening and, as a result, may simply conduct an information interview with you, after which your file goes into a drawer rather than upstairs to someone who counts.

You can also start interviewing higher up the ladder, but this, too, can backfire. If you go over your prospective boss's head, even inadvertently, it will do wonders for your ego (Who doesn't want to chat with the CEO or a division manager?), but it may not advance your cause in the long run, and it may hurt it. The Big Boss may see this as a courtesy interview, and like the human resources person, may not think to mention you to the right person. And if you are handed on by someone with more power than the person who will be your boss, this may create either pressure or resentment in the person who is responsible for hiring you. In other words, your loyalty may be suspect.

It is important, therefore, to find out exactly who has the power to hire you for the job you want and to speak to that person as early as possible in the interviewing process. There is another reason you need to get in to see the person with the power to hire you, and that is because there are two kinds of job openings. There is, on the one hand, the job opening that everyone knows about, the one that has been announced by the company. And there is, on the other hand, the job opening that hasn't been announced because it's still a gleam in some executive's eye. It doesn't officially exist yet. A CEO, for example, has been thinking that he needs another body in top management, someone to stand between him and his line managers. He hasn't thought through his needs yet, so he hasn't mentioned this to the chairman of the board, nor has he mentioned it to any of his line managers. But then, *voila*, you appear on his doorstep one day wearing your best navy pinstripe suit, resume in hand. Suddenly, things click. You are the right person for the job—he knows it, and you know it. Soon, a job has been created where none existed before. But, and this is a very important *but*, that job can't be created unless the right two people—perfect job candidate and perfect prospective boss—meet one another.

THREE STEPS TO GETTING THE RIGHT INTERVIEW WITH THE RIGHT PERSON

A lot of skill, strategic maneuvering, and no small degree of art goes into getting in to see the right interviewer. The three most important things you can do to ensure that you meet Mr. or Ms. Right Boss when you need him or her are, one, to develop a solid network of contacts who will help you; two, to answer the right kinds of ads for the right kinds of jobs; and, three, to let some experts help you. None of these things can be done overnight. You must lay some groundwork. And the ideal time to set things in motion is long before you begin actively looking for a job.

Step One: Laying the Groundwork for Contacts

Maintain a high profile. Maintaining a high profile does two things for you: It makes people see you as executive material, and it will make people recommend you when the right job comes along. The best way to maintain a high profile is to network. Join groups—professional and social—and become active in them. Run for high office or manage a big project, preferably one that will receive lots of publicity. It never hurts to belong to the right clubs, either, and then to involve yourself enough to receive regular mention in their newsletters or other publications. Maintain memberships in alumni and trade associations.

Pay special attention to professional groups, though, because recruiters and prospective employers will start looking in these circles when they have a position to fill. If at all possible, make sure your name is associated with one or more active, powerful professional associations.

Another way to maintain a high profile is to get your name in print. Always list your name in directories when asked to do so. Give interviews to trade journals and business newspapers. When you are promoted or do something worth noting in your present job, send announcements to the local and trade press.

Make sure your name appears in newspaper columns and in industry newspapers and magazines. If possible, get a listing in the *Who's Who* book for your profession. The latter is not as hard to arrange as you might imagine. Getting in the *Who's Who* isn't so easy, but getting into one of the countless books organized by profession is relatively easy. Usually, in fact, the publisher comes to you once you have reached a certain level of achievement. If he doesn't, order the book one year and see if that doesn't bring a biography form and a request to list yourself. Call up the publisher and ask if you can recommend some people. When they send you the form, recommend yourself. Or simply call up the publisher and ask what you have to do to be listed.

Get published, if it will help. In some professions, engineering, for example, you must publish. If yours is a profession where publishing provides recognition, then publish you must. But that's not the end of it. Once you are published, make sure that your article or book falls into the hands of those who might help you. Send a copy of your publication, along with a brief note, to anyone who might find it interesting—and to anyone who will find watching your career interesting, too.

The point of all this is to get yourself noticed by the people who can help you when it's time to job hunt. Getting noticed leads to being recommended. As one executive searcher noted, "People who just sit in an ivory tower and are not known to anyone don't get recommended for the big jobs. They may be the most brilliant and the most skilled people around, but if they aren't out there making themselves visible, people won't even think of them for the top slots. Lots of those people never make it to the very top jobs and don't really understand why."

When recruiters start a search, they often get on the phone to people in their network of professional associations, alumni groups, and trade associations and ask them for recommendations. They read corporate reports and "Who's Who" columns in financial newspapers. If your name keeps popping up over and over again, you begin to look like a good prospect.

When you start to job hunt actively, use your contacts. Some experts estimate that nine of every ten jobs are gotten through one sort of contact or another.

Most people don't realize how many contacts they have until they actually list them. It even helps to divide the master list into A, B, and C lists. A-list people are those who owe you a favor or have a serious personal interest in you. B-list contacts are good professional and social acquaintances who can be called upon to help. C-listers are business acquaintances and casual professional contacts who can help you. These can be almost anyone you have the nerve to approach.

Decide what kind of contacts you have. Regardless of whether someone is on your A, B, or C list, contacts usually are one of three types. There are Matchmakers, Nervous Nellies, and Powerbrokers.

Matchmakers love making matches. They will always help

you sell your skills, recommend you for a job, and tell you when there is going to be an opening. The only problem is that they aren't always discriminating. A matchmaker may love you (and his matchmaking prowess) so much that he'll oversell you to someone. He will make you sound so good that the person he is selling you to wonders why you have to look for a job. If you are as great as the matchmaker says, he'll think, then you should already be a CEO. Matchmakers also may give you weak leads, false leads, or leads that are beneath you. Once in a while, though, a matchmaker hits the jackpot and puts you onto something really great, so keep him or her informed.

Nervous Nellies are the opposite of matchmakers. They are too cautious ever to give you or anyone a glowing recommendation. They don't know whether you're good unless they have worked with you, and even then they tend to be overcritical. A Nervous Nellie will never be aggressive on your behalf or mention a job opening to you before it is advertised.

If a Nervous Nellie ever does tell you about a job, your best bet is to take matters into your own hands. Ask him whom you should talk to and how you can get in touch with that person. Don't leave your fate in the hands of this insecure person. As for any real job leads, you can entirely discount Nervous Nellies. Well, almost entirely—after all, accidents do happen.

A **Powerbroker** is the very best kind of contact anyone can cultivate. A Powerbroker has real power and enjoys wielding it. Like most people, he feels especially good when he can wield it in someone else's behalf. Best of all, though, Powerbrokers have an innate sense about when someone is good at a job. They have an unerring eye for talent, and they believe in their choices. Powerbrokers also like making deals and generally are good at it. A Powerbroker will recommend you for a job and present your case well. He will tell you about a job before it is advertised. You do have to impress a Powerbroker and stay on his good side: he won't squander his power on someone unless he thinks that person is worth the effort.

Use your contacts as much as possible. Ideally, contacts should be cultivated long before you start to job hunt. Keeping in touch with them should be an ongoing process. Let your ex-bosses and ex-colleagues know what you're doing professionally. Keep in touch with professors and academic deans who might have the power to help you. Use holiday cards, an occasional phone call, or the publication of an article or book as occasions to update these professional friends on your life. If you court your contacts properly, they will always be ready to help you.

The ultimate way to be sure that a contact will help you, of course, is to have helped him in the past. If someone owes you a favor, you're much more likely to get a favor back when you need it.

Step Two: Answer Advertisements

Although answering ads may seem like the least likely way for an executive to get a job, it is one more base to cover. Only 15 percent of all job placements involve middlemen. That means a lot of employers and employees must meet each other through advertisements. Needless to say, you won't study the "Help Wanted" columns, but will instead peruse large boxed ads in the business sections of major newspapers and trade newspapers and journals.

Some words of warning: While ads connect you with a prospective employer, they shouldn't be regarded as a reliable source of information. To begin with, don't believe the job description. The responsibilities of the job may be inflated or some important job function may be omitted. When you go into an interview obtained because you responded to an ad, forget the ad and conduct the interview as if you know little about the job and must learn as much as you possibly can. Of course, you should still have done some background research about the company, if not the job, so you can use it to impress the interviewer with your interest.

Also note that the fact that few ads are accurately written or descriptive of the job means that you can pretty safely answer ads even if you don't exactly fit all the qualifications.

Blind ads, where the prospective employer identifies itself only by a box number, are usually a waste of time and are sometimes downright harmful. Your resume sent in response to a blind ad may well land on the wrong person's desk or on the desk of someone who isn't discreet enough to respect your need for confidentiality. Answering the wrong blind ad may result in the news of your job hunt being blasted to your entire professional world—or worse, being whispered to your present employer.

A less important reason to bypass blind ads is that you often don't get a response anyway, so they are wasted effort. This is partly because of the motives of the company running a blind ad. There may be good reasons behind a blind ad, but more often than not, a company is on a fishing expedition ("Let's see who's looking for a job these days"), attempting to weed out minorities and women, or is in the process of raking an employee over the coals by seeking a replacement for him without first telling him or firing him. Companies that resort to blind ads also may be obsessed with secrecy.

Admittedly, some good companies use blind ads, but often their ads are written in such a way that you can read between the lines and figure out who they are anyway. Those are the blind ads you might consider answering.

Step Three: Let the Experts Help You

The third route to obtaining an executive interview is through the experts. Among the experts who are willing and even eager to help an executive find a better job than the one he has are management consultants, image consultants, outplacement specialists, and executive recruiters. Of these experts, the most holy is the executive recruiter.

MANAGEMENT CONSULTANTS   Management consultants who counsel job seekers and run seminars on job-hunting skills abound, and it's sometimes difficult to get a fix on who is a serious consultant and who is merely calling himself a consultant while he looks for a "real" job. One litmus test is how long the person has been in business. Another is how impressive his list of clients is. If a consultant does a lot of consulting work for Fortune 500 companies or major corporations in your industry, that's a good sign. Before you use a consultant's services, ask to see his resume and sit down and talk with him informally about who he knows and what he's done. If he hasn't been a consultant for at least a year, forget him. For your purposes, you want someone with an established, recognized reputation.

The advantage of working with management consultants is that they frequently work both sides of the fence. A consultant may be counseling job candidates on how to interview while at the same time counseling employers on how to hire good employees. Most management consultants limit themselves to helping you brush up on your job-hunting skills and do not do any direct placement. They typically conduct seminars or short classes on job-hunting skills, and many do individual counseling. But keep in mind that some consultants may have contacts that can be very helpful to you.

IMAGE CONSULTANTS Image consultants, like management consultants, usually do not do any direct placement. In fact, an image consultant, unlike a management consultant, may not even have any contacts that will help you get a job. Instead, these specialists work with you to improve your image so you will be clearly and easily identifiable as top executive material.

Image consultants provide a range of services, and they are often fairly specialized. One consultant may advise clients only on how to dress; another may work only on a client's speech; while still another may teach power body language.

The worst way to find out whether you need an image consultant is to ask one. In an image consultant's eyes, everybody can do with a little polishing. The best way to find out whether you can use professional help is to ask a friend, after first explaining your fears and beseeching the friend to give you an honest opinion. Once a friend is convinced that an honest opinion is truly sought, most will oblige with the truth.

To choose a good image consultant, first meet with him or her to be sure you get along personally. Once you begin working with a consultant, don't let him or her undermine you. You are there because you need some build-up, and the most effective way for someone to give you this is to be totally supportive. Unfortunately, many people don't consider using a consultant until they have lost a job. Their morale is low, and their self-esteem needs a boost. So they decide to let an expert "remake" them. Image consultants who undermine their clients—either subtly or not so subtly—do more damage than good in the long run.

Before signing on with an image consultant, ask for references, and then check those references carefully. Find out if past clients felt they were truly helped by the service. Did they get the service they were promised? Did the assistance have a lasting effect? Do they think the work they did with the consultant contributed to their getting a better job? Would they spend the same amount of money again for the advice they got? If the answer is yes to most of these questions, and if you feel the chemistry is right with the image consultant, then go ahead and sign on for the help at your own risk.

Management and image consultants provide the least measurable return for your investment of any of the experts you can turn to. In addition, their fees are often high—running anywhere from hundreds to thousands of dollars—and, unfortunately, what they charge may have little or no relation to the quality of their service. Before you sign on for a consultant, therefore, you should ask yourself whether this is a service you really need or whether you might seek better assistance elsewhere.

OUTPLACEMENT SPECIALISTS   Another kind of expert who helps job-seeking executives are outplacement specialists. These are employment specialists who step in when an executive has been fired or otherwise displaced to help him find a new position. The cost of outplacement counseling is high—as much as $10,000 per executive—and the company often foots the bill. Outplacement specialists who work for companies and are paid by them usually do not take on "retail trade," to use their term for individual clients who do not come through a company. Retail-trade specialists can be hired by individual clients, although the price is still high, and, as is the case with management and image consultants, the price doesn't necessarily bear any relation to the quality of service provided. A few firms, though, do both kinds of outplacement counseling and do it very well. Many outplacement counselors also do executive placement.

Since few people emerge from a firing with their egos intact, it is important to work with a good outplacement specialist. You need someone who will help you pick up the pieces and glue them back together. With an outplacement counselor, as with these other experts, chemistry is essential. Companies that use outplacement specialists often rely on more than one firm, so if you don't like the atmosphere or the counselor you see at one firm, ask about another one. The same applies if you are buying your own outplacement counseling: Be sure you like the atmosphere and the people with whom you will be working. Always get and check out references before signing on for any outplacement counseling on your own.

A good outplacement firm must have a program that can be tailored to your needs. For example, if you write a crack resume but have trouble interviewing, then you don't need an outplacement firm that will make you rewrite your resume to their taste but counsels you very little on interviewing techniques. You need one that will help you do some role-playing or other "practice" for interviews. A good outplacement firm should also have a library, word processing equipment, videotape machines, and a place for you to work when you're in their offices. Finally, and perhaps most valuable, a good outplacement firm should also temper its enthusiasm with reality. The people shouldn't tell you that getting another job will be a snap if you have suffered a serious career setback or have some actual handicaps that will make getting another job difficult.

EXECUTIVE RECRUITERS   The last and certainly the most important kind of expert is the executive recruiter, also known as the executive searcher or headhunter. At the very top level, you do not go to an executive recruiter; he or she comes to you. But as you will see, there are ways to get them to come to you.

All headhunters, whether they will admit it or not, constantly need new blood. Top executive recruiters love to cultivate the image that you can't get to them. "We get fifteen thousand resumes a year," one recruiter commented with great pride, "and they're all read at the clerical level." But that is not exactly the case. Not only can you get to them, there are some very specific ways of doing just that.

Your goal is to get to know an executive recruiter who can then be used as another contact. You want either to get listed in a recruiter's data bank or, better yet, to cultivate a personal relationship with a recruiter so he will come to you when he has a job for which you are qualified. You should aim for the top firms in major placement cities such as New York, Chicago, and San Francisco. The major firms in these cities make placements for companies all over the world, and many maintain offices in many cities.

As noted earlier, maintaining a high profile is the best way to get noticed by an executive recruiter. Contacts also help. If someone you know has been placed by a search firm, he or she has some entree with them, and a recruiter may see you, if only as a favor to your friend or colleague.

Another way to meet a good recruiter—one that requires more effort—is to hand-select him and then court him just as you would any other job contact. Start courting a recruiter long before you think you will need his services. Al Duarte had some ideas about how to court a recruiter: "The trouble is that most people send a resume to a recruiter when they're looking for a job. That is the worst time to do it. It's far better to get to know the recruiter beforehand, try to develop some rapport. The chances that a recruiter will be working on an assignment that will fit your background at the time you really need a job are pretty slim, so it's best to get to know that recruiter, let his firm get to know you, and get into their files, which are always up-to-date."

Duarte suggests: "Call up the recruiter and say you would like to come by and say hello. That doesn't always work because recruiters are busy people, but try other little, even simple, things. Try marketing yourself, if you want to call it that.

"When we're developing clients, if we see an article on the chemical industry, we'll clip that article and send it along to someone we know at a chemical company we would like to do placement for. A would-be candidate can do the same thing with a recruiter. Clip an article and send it with a note saying that you thought he might be interested. Next time, you can say to him, 'By the way, here's my resume. I'm not looking and don't want anything right now, but down the road, who knows?'"

John Foster at Boyden Associates, Incorporated, an executive search firm, reports that most firms will make an effort to interview someone who sends a resume and is highly placed even if there isn't a job at the time.

Cultivating a headhunter is only the first step, though. You also have to know how to deal with him when he does come knocking at your door.

·| *FOUR* |·
What to Do When the Headhunter Calls

Sooner or later, if you have reached the upper management ranks, maintained a high profile, and networked yourself in your "spare time," the telephone will ring, you will answer it, and on the other end of the line will be a headhunter asking if you have any interest in interviewing for another—and usually better—job than the one you presently hold.

You will give the stock answer: You are pretty happy where you are, but you're never adverse to hearing about an interesting job, so you are willing to talk to him. You should be willing to talk to a recruiter even if you are happy where you are, and you should tell a recruiter you're happy where you are even if you're dying to get out because you will never look more desirable to a recruiter than when you are happily employed and have to be wooed away to a new position. Prospective employers, too, find this an attractive stance in a job candidate, particularly at the managerial level. Thus, you should always play a little hard to get when dealing with an executive recruiter and his client.

You also need to be somewhat guarded when a recruiter calls. There will be, of necessity, some mystery attached to your very early dealings with even the best executive recruiter (he won't tell you who the client is, for example), and you should not commit to anything until you have checked him out.

First check out whether this is someone with whom you want to have a relationship. In other words, is this a bona fide executive recruiter, someone reliable and ethical whom you can trust, or is this a fly-by-night operator, unscrupulous and possibly unethical? The latter, unfortunately, abound in the world of job placement. The worst ones work out of telephone booths and have no real relationship with prospective employers other than a loose agreement that they will look at any resumes the recruiter submits. Such "recruiters" (if that word can be applied here) basically answer ads just like anyone else, only they submit other people's resumes. Then they expect a fee when someone is hired, usually from the employer but sometimes from the person they claim to have placed. They may have a company's okay to look for someone to fill a job, but they are not hired exclusively for a fee by a client firm to search for a list of suitable job candidates the way an executive recruiter is.

These flesh peddlers have even been known to do some serious damage on occasion. One woman reported her experience with this kind of recruiter: "A legitimate recruiter whom I had contacted had a job lead in a bank and sent them my resume. The bank called and said they already had my resume from another recruiter. Months earlier, I had contacted a recruiter by mail. I'd never heard from him even though I had enclosed a copy of my resume. Nearly a year later, he sent my resume out to this bank without my knowledge, obviously. When I called him, he gave me a lot of excuses for why he had done it, but then I found out that he always operates that way. I learned that recruiting can be a dog-eat-dog world, and that I'd have to be more careful."

Never send a resume in response to a phone call. Always wait until you meet a recruiter face-to-face to hand him your resume.

Ask the recruiter to describe the job. Then listen very carefully to what he says. Even a good recruiter won't name a company at this stage, but he should be able to describe the size of the company, its location, and its industry. Get a written description of the job from him. It should be a page or more long and should describe the duties, functions, and responsibilities of the person required, the qualifications that are sought in job candidates, and a description of the company. It should not be skimpy.

Ask to call the recruiter back at his office. Then do so, and pay attention to such things as whether a secretary or an answering service answers, whether there is noise in the background (in other words, are you calling a public phone booth or a low-rent, shared office?), and whether you are treated courteously. High-quality recruiters hire high-quality people to work for them, and you will be treated courteously and even with great respect when you call the office.

Always meet with a recruiter before deciding to work with him. A legitimate recruiter will expect to meet with you in person, and if you live in another city, will pay for your transportation and expenses to and from the meeting so you can be interviewed in person. (The client actually picks up the tab.)

If you are trying to cultivate a recruiter, and the offices are in a different city, a recruiter obviously won't pay you to fly in for an interview. And you shouldn't let him think you have flown in just to meet him, even if you have. Your best bet is to try to cultivate four or five top recruiters in a nearby city and then, when things have progressed to a certain level with all the recruiters, to take a few days to visit the city and call on all of them. You should realize that this could either work well or end in total disaster. It is possible that none of the recruiters will be interested or able to book an appointment with you when you plan your foray.

Finally, you should be realistic about whether your career is far enough along for a top-level executive recruiter to be contacting you. If you're basically still in middle management, it's wise to be leery of anyone who calls you and has a dynamite, very high-level position to offer you. Elite headhunters don't usually deal with middle managers. There are, however, some good middle-management executive recruiters around. They are a stepping stone to the more elite executive recruiters. While the names of the top recruiting firms are well-known to most people who read the business press, many of the middle-level recruiters are independents or are less well-known. There is no reason not to work with these people once you have carefully checked out their references.

How Recruiters Operate

Once you decide to work with a recruiter, your relations will go more smoothly if you understand how recruiters operate.

A recruiter conducts a complete search for every assignment. Sometimes, he can pull someone from the data bank his firm maintains, and quite often, the client will provide the recruiter with a list of "target" companies to raid, if possible, for talent.

The typical recruiter handles very few assignments at any one time. Six to eight appears to be the average load. Executive recruiters can afford to be this selective for two reasons: first, they are well paid by their clients, and second, executive recruiters generally handle only people in middle and top management. (Middle-management searches are those in the $35,000 to $80,000 total compensation range, and top-management searches are those in the $80,000-plus total compensation range. The average range of placement the last few years has been the $90,000 to $100,000 total compensation package.)

What all this basically means is that you won't find it very helpful to go to a recruiter when *you* want to change jobs. The chances that he or she will be working on an assignment that can use your specific talents at the time you want to change are slim.

Another important thing you must understand is the absolute care with which executive recruiters operate with regard to their clients. Recruiters sometimes court a client for months or even years before receiving an assignment. And all the recruiters interviewed for this book were unanimous in saying that the worst thing they could do on a search is to send the wrong candidate to the client. One recruiter's statement only echoed that of other recruiters when he said, "Sending out the wrong job candidate means we haven't done our job. We haven't understood our client's needs."

To avoid sending out the wrong person for the job, a recruiter takes several precautions.

A recruiter is sometimes tougher about choosing a job candidate than a client would be. One experienced job hunter who had risen through the ranks, and in doing so had also worked her way up through the ranks of executive recruiters, said, "The interviewing only gets tougher the higher up you go, when you would think your credentials and experience would speak for themselves. A lot of recruiters will grill you, go through your entire life with you step-by-step, attempt to find out whether you adored your father and what other heroes you had, ask you a lot about how you spend your leisure time, and, in general, spend a lot of time going over irrelevant things that have little to do with your qualifications for the job. They do this just to make sure they've got the right person, to make sure that they know everything about the person."

You should keep in mind, however, that although executive recruiters err on the side of the overly cautious, they are also among the toughest and best interviewers around, and you must know how to handle them to get past them.

A recruiter will also check your references—and anything

else you say—very carefully. Lots of employers still don't bother to check references, but a headhunter will do some scouting around to find out if you really did everything you said you did, and if you did it, he'll find out whether you did it alone, as you claim, or whether your role was actually smaller than you have admitted.

A recruiter will also check out your compensation package carefully, although he usually knows whether you are leveling with him without checking. Unlike prospective employers, who rarely interview and may have only a vague impression of what the competition pays its management employees, the recruiter talks to executives and managers all the time. He knows what the typical range of pay is at various levels, what different industries pay, and he has finely tuned antennae that help him sense when an interviewee is not leveling with him about compensation—or anything else, for that matter.

HOW TO MAKE THE MOST OF YOUR MEETING WITH THE RECRUITER

At some point, you will meet personally with the executive recruiter who calls you. This meeting will take place even if you must take a day or two off work and travel across country for it. You would do the same for a potential employer who was interested in you, and you should do the same for an executive recruiter who may have a job for you.

Go into the meeting as relaxed as possible. That will impress the recruiter. In describing the initial interview with a job candidate or someone who is being interviewed as a prospective job candidate, John Foster said, "Usually it's on a first-name basis right from the start. I try to make the setting as informal as possible. There's a myth that the recruiter is going to put the candidate through all sorts of stress. That just doesn't happen. The candidate and recruiter meet as equals. Before a person goes into the search business, he's usually done something significant and knows how to run a business, how businesses are organized, and something about business ethics. A good recruiter is mostly interested in examining the candidate's record, looking at how he did things, and what has been required to accomplish certain things. That's what the initial meeting and any other meetings are all about."

Recruiters agree there are no rules about where a meeting will take place. One recruiter noted, "Often I invite someone here to the office first and then go on to lunch. I might do the preliminary paperwork in the office, so I'm not writing a lot during lunch and attracting attention that way. Lunch is more personal. It's social and one-to-one. I can find out what really makes the person tick. The more time I can spend getting to know someone, obviously, the better it is for my client."

When you have lunch with a recruiter, realize that your social skills are being evaluated. The recruiter wants to know that you can handle a knife and fork with skill, and that you don't break under the stress of dealing with a snobbish maitre d' hote. One recruiter admitted, in fact, that his only stress test was to ask a job candidate to meet him in a busy, midtown Manhattan restaurant with a notoriously rude headwaiter. He tells his guest he will make a reservation. He also tells his guest to be shown to his table, something this particular maitre d' hote hates to do. The recruiter always walks in ten minutes late. He considers the mental state of the candidate something of an acid test. If the candidate has rolled with the punches and says little or nothing about the headwaiter's treatment or comments only jokingly, the recruiter figures the person is easygoing enough to deal with a pressure situation. If the candidate is furious and can't let go of how he has been treated, the recruiter knows he has an anxious, perhaps overbearing person on his hands. Such a person, he feels, wouldn't stand up well to on-the-job pressures if a headwaiter could throw him or her so easily.

Presumably, if you are an executive, you won't have trouble lunching with a recruiter, and recruiters report that few executives lack the social skills to pass this small test. Mostly, they all emphasized, lunch just provided an opportunity to get to know the candidate a little bit better and to talk, perhaps, on a more personal level.

Most executives even pass the time-honored test of whether or not to drink at lunch, according to many recruiters. One recruiter said that it was rare for anyone to order anything strong to drink at lunch these days, and all agreed that in this age of health and fitness obsessiveness, candidates are as likely to refuse a drink as to order one. But as long as the candidate didn't down two whiskeys on the rocks over lunch or show an inability to handle a small amount of liquor, no recruiter objected to a candidate having a drink with lunch.

The dress rules are a little trickier for a recruiter interview than for a regular job interview. Most executives pass the dress test quite well, according to the recruiters interviewed for this book. It seems that by the time a headhunter calls, most managers know how to dress like an executive.

In general, dress for an interview with a recruiter exactly as you would for any job interview (see Chapter 10). But there are occasions when this rule should be broken. If you meet with a recruiter over a weekend when you would not normally be wearing work clothes, then wear casual clothes. You should do this to show that you are equals, even to flex your power a little bit, and to avoid the appearance of being stiff. (In fact, under these circumstances, it's okay if the recruiter shows up in work clothes while you are wearing casual clothes.)

Some words of warning, though: Show up in quality casual

clothes, long pants and/or a skirt and a tweed blazer, for example. Unless you are meeting at a club where you have been actively engaged in a sport and have a legitimate reason to be wearing active sports clothes, don't wear a leotard, sweatsuit, warm-up clothes, or any kind of active sports clothes unless you want to risk looking silly. If you're unsure of your social skills, *Executive Etiquette* (St. Martin's Press) by Marjabelle Young Stewart and Marian Faux or *The New Office Etiquette* (Poseidan) by George Mazzei offer a refresher course.

Talk openly and honestly with the recruiter. He'll probe and check you out so carefully that he'll find any skeletons in the closet anyway, so your best bet is to impress him with your directness and bring up a problem area before he has a chance to uncover it. (There are limitations to this, of course, and you don't want to be self-destructive. If you resigned under pressure from a company, but you know the recruiter will never find out the real story, then don't, for example, confess that you officially resigned but were, in effect, fired.)

The recruiter will usually examine your resume carefully and may go through it with you step-by-step, seeking to fill in any obvious gaps and to ferret out any that aren't so obvious. John Foster reported, "During the course of this kind of conversation, centered around a resume, I can usually find out a great deal about a person. I can certainly decide whether I think the person is worth moving on to the client or perhaps not sending him to the client but sticking him in our data bank."

The biggest mistake you can make with an interviewer at this stage is to be dishonest. He will check your references, and most recruiters are good enough at what they do to sniff out problem areas even before they do this. One recruiter noted, "If a candidate is vague with me and talks less about one job than another, I'll probe that job he isn't talking about. Did he have a boss he didn't like? Was he asked to resign? Is there a reason he only worked there for a year? I can smell it, and I usually sniff it out."

Duarte agrees that dishonesty is the worst mistake a job candidate can make. He commented, "A recruiter is very embarrassed if the client learns something about a candidate that the recruiter did not. Maybe I'm being too idealistic, but I think the candidate should be honest almost to the point of volunteering something the recruiter missed. This is a situation where you will work together, and if you try to snow the recruiter, well, most of us have been around too long for that to work."

The one area where you should be a little less direct is when discussing salary. Obviously, you want to earn as much as you can. And while a middleman can be helpful in this regard, he can also hold you back—primarily by telling a prospective employer who's willing to pay $85,000 for someone that you can be had for $60,000. Try to avoid this situation by stating what your "entire package" is worth rather than naming just your salary. Or say you're looking for something in the "range of" and name a range. Say you missed one raise because of company reorganization or economic policy (whatever is plausible) and will have another raise coming up in two months (if this is true), so to cover these raises, you would have to have X amount of money. Don't waste your time inflating your salary, though, because with the recruiter's experience, he or she can usually pinpoint your earnings within a thousand dollars.

HOW TO IMPRESS A HEADHUNTER

Always remember the cardinal rule of attracting an executive recruiter: He wants to think you are happily employed. Let him think this, and let him think you must be wooed away. There are additional ways to impress the recruiter:

Be tight with your time when setting up an appointment.
Most executives are busy people. Very busy people. You should
be no exception, even if you're dying to see a recruiter and quite
sure you want the job he's handling. Without being excessive,
flash around your busy schedule a little bit before you settle on
a time to meet. Say something like, "Tuesday's out, I'm in Atlanta that day. Wednesday morning I've got a big meeting
scheduled in the office, and Wednesday night, I'm going to
Washington. Friday, I'm in my office but booked solid. But
wait a minute. Here's a break! How about Friday at five-thirty?"

When you do meet with a recruiter, don't oversell yourself.
There is a difference between an interview with a prospective
employer and an interview with an executive recruiter, even
though both are means to the same end.

With a prospective employer, you need to display energy and
enthusiasm along with your qualifications. A recruiter, though,
looks for something else: quiet self-confidence. Anxiety will
hurt with a recruiter. So will eagerness, if it is perceived to be
anxiety.

Let the recruiter sell you. Let him or her peruse your resume
and ask about your achievements. When asked, don't act overly
enthusiastic as you explain what you can do and have done.
Resist the urge to launch into a full-scale sales pitch. Stop talking when you have explained something fully enough.

If you can mention another achievement that is related to the
one you were asked about, say something such as: "There's
something else you ought to know in connection with that."
Avoid saying the kinds of things you would say in an interview
with a prospective employer, such as: "What else can I tell you
about myself?" "Are there any other things you would like to
discuss?" or "I'd like to tell you what I consider to be my most
important achievement." Let the recruiter probe. Especially at
this initial interviewing stage, you still need to maintain the
stance of a person who is happily employed elsewhere.

When discussing your references, if you had a bad experience with a former employer, admit it. Be forthright about saying, "Frankly, I don't know what kind of references you will get from her about me. We had our differences, and we certainly had different approaches to managing. I learned a lot from her, but it was always a trying relationship. I do know that you will get good references from this person and this person." See what you have done? You have admitted to a problem, stated it in positive terms, and then directed his attention to something far more positive. This makes you look good.

Mention your favorite participant sport. This shows that you are competitive, and it shows that you are physically fit. In today's world, physical fitness counts for a lot. If you've got it, flaunt it. It will impress the recruiter; it will impress prospective employers.

Mention something you have read lately. This doesn't mean the latest spy novel or western that you read on the beach last summer. Mention an article in *Fortune, The Wall Street Journal, The New York Times,* or *Time* or *Newsweek.* Refer to a book you have read, preferably a business book, such as *The Pursuit of Excellence, Corporate Cultures,* or one of the books on how the Japanese are better managers than Americans are. Or, if you really want to impress, mention reading a book on how the Japanese aren't really such good managers and how good-old-American know-how is actually where it's at, after all. This will balance out your comments about sports and show off your intellectual side.

You end the meeting. You be the one who has to get back to work or go to another meeting. This makes you look busy and powerful; and best of all, you look happily employed.

HOW NOT TO IMPRESS A HEADHUNTER

Don't waste his time. It's perfectly acceptable and even desirable for you to make time to talk to any good executive recruiter who contacts you. You should state that you're happy where you are and don't think you're seriously looking around. He will still want to see you and, at this stage, you should still see him. Let him interview you, get to know you, and even give you an evaluation of your worth in the marketplace. *But if you still don't want to change jobs, end it here.* Never let a recruiter send you out on interviews if you aren't serious about changing jobs.

Be honest with a recruiter about your limitations once he has described the job to you. As Duarte said, "If a company happens to be located in Rochester, New York, and you've got an invalid mother you can't leave in New York City, don't go on a fact-finding interview. You can't move. Put it up front. You hurt yourself with the recruiter if you don't. And you don't want to do that. The recruiter will never contact you again if you've led him on like that."

Don't use a recruiter to change careers. They like a sure thing. They are, in fact, paid to find a sure thing. As Millie McCoy noted: "Clients pay us to find a track record of success in their industry or in a more sophisticated industry than theirs. They don't pay us to take someone out of a mature industry and put him into a high-tech industry, because the cultures are so different. If someone is going to transfer from one field to another, it is better to do this on his own and with his own contacts."

HOW THE RECRUITER CAN HELP YOU GET THAT JOB

Once you have made the grade with an executive recruiter, there is a lot he or she can—and will—do to help you snare the job.

He will coach you for the interview. He'll do this by telling you about the company and the person or persons whom you will be seeing when you go for an interview with the client. One recruiter described how the information divulged at this stage involves both professional and personal facts about the prospective employer: "When the time comes to reveal who the client is, we spend a lot of time coaching the job candidate about who the client is, what he does, and why we think he is the person most qualified for the job. We talk about personalities, whether the client plays tennis or some other sport, where he went to school, what his pet charities are, even the clubs he belongs to—anything that will help establish rapport and make the interview go well."

Another recruiter said: "You always want a candidate to go into an interview as well-versed as possible. He should know as much as he possibly can, and very often, the better candidates will call and say, 'I don't understand this section of the annual report.' We'll try to amplify it for him. Sometimes, though, I'll have to say that I don't have the answer, and that this would make a very good question to ask during the interview. We counsel people to ask as many questions as possible during the interview."

The recruiter will provide background information. This can save you hours in the library and time otherwise spent tracking down information on a company you're about to interview with. A recruiter will give you an annual report, stockholder's reports, 10-Ks, and other background data. One tip: Ask for still more material than you are given. One recruiter recalled being especially impressed with a job candidate who asked her for short biographies of the top executives of a firm where he would be interviewing.

The recruiter will play the role of middleman during the job negotiations. Duarte described the recruiter's role in this respect: "We try to act as the middleman. We can try to get the parties together without having a confrontation, without either an offer or a request going on the table that is going to embarrass the other party. I can tell the candidate that I think his salary expectations are unreasonable, but I'll feel the client out. On the other hand, I can also tell the client who is going to offer X dollars that the candidate will walk away from that offer. I can get both parties to be a little more realistic."

Never forget, though, that recruiters are of necessity more on the client's side than on your side in any salary negotiations. Depending upon how close the recruiter is to the client, he or she will sometimes tell a client when a job candidate can be gotten for a ridiculously low amount, and they will also tell a client when he's about to pay too much. Generally, the recruiter can be more helpful to the job candidate with other forms of compensation and perks, mostly because he's got little to lose there and can even help himself. A client will be justifiably angry if he spends $20,000 more than necessary to hire someone, but he'll consider the recruiter helpful who can suggest the perks that will win over a desirable candidate.

Recruiters provide confidentiality. By using a recruiter, a company can conduct a search anonymously and confidentially. But more important, and often overlooked, is the fact that you may need to look for a job in secrecy. A good recruiter won't reveal who you are to the client until he is sure you are interested in the job and are a viable candidate for it.

A recruiter knows whereof he speaks when he counsels you. Unlike many other experts, the executive recruiter is often taken into the client's confidence and knows the parameters of the job he is handling. He or she knows, for example, whether his client will consider someone who has a firing on his record or whether the client will hire someone who's controversial. And most recruiters will be frank with you about the fact that you aren't right for the job, thus saving you time and energy.

An executive recruiter can provide a debriefing. Although few candidates ask for one, a recruiter often can tell you exactly why you didn't get a job. Sometimes, he doesn't know the real reason, but if he knows why you weren't hired, he is often willing to share that information with you on request. Skilled interviewer that he is, he is even likely to describe the reasons in a way that will be constructive to you in future job hunts.

But don't let your guard down too much. However much the recruiter may appear to be on your side (and he will seem to be) as he prepares you for the big interview, you must understand that he or she is constantly evaluating you. He asks himself such questions as: Have I missed something important about this person? Can he or she bear up under the scrutiny of the CEO or whoever will be involved in the hiring process? Does this person make as good an impression as I think he or she does?

If you do bare your innermost thoughts to a recruiter, you run the risk that he will develop second thoughts about you, depending upon how you handle the situation. He will, for example, give you advice on how to explain a touchy resignation, but he doesn't want to hear that you were traumatized when your resignation was asked for and have never quite regained your self-confidence. He also may act on those thoughts and rule you out at the last minute as a viable candidate. If he does this, he will have no qualms about picking up the telephone, even after he has recommended you to the client, and informing the client that he doesn't think you're quite right for the job, after all. Whether it's genuine or not, you have to present the same facade of self-confidence and enthusiasm to the recruiter that you will present during the executive interview.

Basically, an executive recruiter expects a job candidate to walk into his or her office a fully blown executive. He wants you to know how to talk, eat, dress, project, and otherwise present yourself. If you need help with any of this, see a career or an image consultant. You won't get to first base with an executive recruiter if you're not already cast in the right mold when you cross his threshold.

·| FIVE |·

Homework: The Key to a Smooth Interview

If there is one thing that employers, executive recruiters, human resources people, and outplacement specialists are all in complete agreement about, it is that far too few job candidates spend enough time preparing for an interview. Of those that bother to prepare, most focus their attention on collecting facts; they don't take the time to devise a list of hard-driving questions that will both impress a prospective employer and put him on the spot so that the candidate can really find out what makes the company tick.

Robert F. Maddocks, vice-president of organization and management resources for RCA, said many candidates don't even take the time to understand the basics about a corporation. According to Maddocks, they often don't read the annual report and the 10-Ks, forms that RCA and most other corporations routinely authorize executive recruiters to release to potential job candidates. Noted Maddocks: "I rarely experience tough, hard questions from candidates. If questions showed an understanding of the corporation, I would welcome them. The kinds of questions I get show the candidate read the newspaper, not anything more. Anybody can ask those kinds of questions. I would welcome tough questions, but I don't get them very often."

Few people seem to comprehend that a successful job interview is very much a two-way street: The company interviews you, and you, sometimes working even harder, interview the company. The idea that a candidate should interview prospective employers strikes some people as strange, particularly those who are especially aware that the interviewer isn't exactly in the driver's seat during an interview. Asking the tough questions, however, has its decided benefits, and in a tight race for a job, it may be *the* factor that sets you apart from the other two or three highly qualified candidates.

HOW TO PREPARE FOR A SUCCESSFUL INTERVIEW

To interview a prospective employer, you need to be very well prepared—overprepared, in fact—because if you do your homework as thoroughly as you should, you will show off only a small percentage of what you know during an interview. You should investigate three general areas before interviewing with a company for whom you think you would like to work.

Area #1: Gathering Background on an Industry

The first step in preparing for an interview is to gather background information about the industry. This is especially valuable if you are attempting to switch from one industry to another. The best way to learn about an industry is to read the industry's trade magazine, *The Wall Street Journal*, *The New York Times*, *Barrons*, and the other major business publications regularly and over an extended period of time. While a minimum of several days is needed to prepare adequately for an interview, even better is to spend several months to a year watching an industry, if possible, before scheduling interviews. Months before you begin job-hunting, start paying attention to industry trends and forecasts. Read the specialized trade magazines of various industries such as *Ad Age*, *Publishers Weekly*, *Plastics*, *Packaging Digest*, *Iron Age*, and *Oil & Gas* to gather even more in-depth knowledge.

As you gather data, try to learn the jargon. While you should never go into an interview and throw around jargon, especially if you've only recently learned it and it's not the industry you work in, knowing some key words, phrases, and acronyms during a job interview has its advantages. For one thing, jargon lets you talk with the person interviewing you in a kind of shorthand. You can cover much more territory than you would if you didn't know the jargon. Jargon is also a way to show that you are interested enough to have done some homework, and, most important, that you have the capacity to master new subjects. A word of warning though, as one seasoned job hunter pointed out: "I only used jargon as much as I was comfortable with, because I knew if someone called me on it, I was in trouble."

Area #2: Gathering Background on a Particular Company

To make the most of an interview, you must familiarize yourself with the employer's products, markets, annual sales, management turnover rate, recent achievements, forecasts, projects, charitable affiliations, problems, and acquisitions and divestitures.

According to Janet Tweed, head of Tweed Gilbert, an executive search and outplacement firm, "A job candidate should take an annual report and a 10-K and devour them. It helps to know a lot about the competition, too. Know what the philosophy of the company is—that's often presented in the president's page of the annual report."

At the initial stages of gathering information about a company, it's also worthwhile to put in a call to your stockbroker or investment analyst. Pick his brain on the company and the industry in general; he watches trends, corporate aggressiveness, turnover, and profits. When you have exhausted your live contacts, head to the library to see what you can find out about the company. Start with the *Business Periodicals Index*. Look for general articles about the industry and specific articles about the company. You're in luck if someone has written a comprehensive profile of the company in the past two or three years. Other places to uncover information about specific companies include the following:

Standard & Poor's Register of Corporations, Directors, and Executives
Fortune's Job Listings
Moody's Manuals and *Moody's News Reports*
Dun & Bradstreet directories
McRae's Blue Book
Standard & Poor's Corporation Records
Value Line Investment Survey

Any major library or college business library will have most of these publications.

Obviously, information is more widely available for companies that are publicly held than for privately held ones. In fact, you may have trouble learning very much about a privately held company. You can turn to more informal sources of information such as present and former employees, if you have the contacts. But you also may have to go into the interview with a little less knowledge and ask questions of the person who interviews you.

Companies provide many clues about themselves and their corporate culture in what they write about themselves and what they permit others to write about them. Therefore, you should read annual reports, paying special attention to the president's letter; interviews in the trade press with management; and even press releases. You may have to read between the lines to uncover attitudes and cultural beliefs, but the extra sleuthing will pay off.

Area #3: Gathering Background on a Company's Corporate Culture

The role of the corporate culture in job placement cannot be underestimated these days. Executive recruiters mentally classify candidates and won't send someone to a company if he or she is not deemed a good cultural match. Prospective employers, especially human resources people, all want to explain their culture to you and, more important, they want you to act as if you understand their culture. So part of doing homework involves boning up on the personality of the company. This kind of information is rarely found in libraries but is more likely to be gathered from your own network contacts.

Some cultures are dominated by a hero. These are especially easy to spot and understand since they are dominated by one personality, usually a founder such as Tom Watson at IBM, Dave Packard at Hewlett-Packard, Helena Rubenstein at her cosmetics company, and Mary Kay Ash at Mary Kay Cosmetics.

Newer cultural heroes are Lee Iacocca at Chrysler and Frank Borman at Eastern Airlines. If you can read something written by or about the hero, you will begin to understand the cultural milieu of the company. For extensive definitions and descriptions of the main kinds of corporate cultures, read *Corporate Cultures: The Rights and Rituals of Corporate Life*, by Terence E. Deal and Allen A. Kennedy (Addison-Wesley, 1982).

Use your knowledge about the corporate culture to sell yourself. An understanding of the culture will help you plan what you say about such things as your job goals, your feelings about your career, and the relationship between your career and your family.

Once you have gotten a fix on the culture of a company, you are on your way to understanding the mentality and personality of the corporate officers, but you should also do some specific research about the persons who are likely to interview you.

Don't ignore the board members, either. If you're lucky, you'll know one or two, and they'll be invaluable contacts for you as you move through the hiring process. If you're using an executive recruiter, he or she will be able to fill you in on the personalities of the people you will be seeing, as well as on their management styles.

In doing this kind of personal research, look for ties you have in common—a shared school, club, or charitable interest. Find out about their career paths and whom they have worked for.

When researching the CEO, the most important thing you can learn about him is his management style. Does he believe in management by objectives or management by participation? Is he supportive and well-liked, or is he a tyrant who is feared and maybe not even respected? Most top executives choose managers who emulate their management style, so if you know the CEO's management style, you know just about everyone's management style in a company.

The best way to get this information, of course, is to talk to people who currently work for, or have worked for, the top managers, especially anyone whom you may be working for. Take what people say with a grain of salt, though, because someone who works for a tough manager may be inclined to rationalize his boss's behavior as a means of surviving, or the employee may even be cut from the same mold and therefore not be the best observer of that management style. Conversely, someone who has left the employment of a particularly difficult manager may paint a bleaker picture of that boss than is actually the case.

Final Tips on Preparing for a Successful Interview

In addition to using inside contacts to learn about the personalities of the people at the company, use personal contacts and the grapevine to find out anything you can about the company. This is the kind of information you should tuck away for future reference—something to verify during an interview and when you do your post-interview intelligence-seeking.

Employees of the firm can be an important source of information. Be grateful if someone other than the hiring executive calls you to confirm an interview date and time. Appointments are often set up by the human resources person, and this can provide you with an opportunity to do still more homework. It is, after all, this person's job to fill you in on the company. But even a lower level executive or manager—someone who knows someone you know or someone you knew from college or business school—can be a gold mine of certain kinds of information.

Save the in-depth questions for the interview and go for general information that doesn't threaten these people. Find out more, for example, about the company's background, how it got started, whether it has any heroes, what makes its products so successful, what the weaknesses and strengths of its management are, and if you can, what kind of employer it is overall. Note: You probably won't get inside information on the kind of place this is to work at from a human resources person (his job, by and large, is to supply you with the party line), but almost any other contact may tell you the real story if you ask for it.

Pay attention to gossip. There is often a kernel of truth in any item of gossip. Is the gossip mostly about the management style of the company? If so, what kinds of things do you hear? Is it a dog-eat-dog place, a place where heads roll when profits are low? Is there a star system, or are team players valued? Gossip about the latest product line is often more accurate than the current company propaganda. In this stage of doing homework, don't discount any bit of information, however minor, until you have had an opportunity to check it out. Store everything away for the day of the interview.

Know when you have done enough. Finally, because your time is valuable, it is important to realize when you have done enough homework on a company—as well as when you are about to go on one of those rare interviews where you don't need to do much homework.

Sometimes, it is important to gather general knowledge about an industry rather than specific knowledge about a company. One university administrator who was attempting to change industries recognized that, on at least one interview, there was little he could tell the prospective employer about how to run his business. The two men had been working closely for several months on a project involving their two businesses, and the job candidate knew how much his prospective employer knew: a lot. He recalled: "In the case of this interview, for a large bookstore operation that was branching out across the country, I took my knowledge of a bookstore operation on my campus and my understanding of the economics of that one and tried to translate that into other types of campuses and the kind of approach that might work on different campuses. This was a first-cut sales job, and if I had gone with this company, I would have gone into a market in a university setting and sold them on why this type of operation would be better for them than their present one.

"My credentials were one selling point; my experience was a second selling point; and my knowledge of this type of lease operation was yet another selling point. So there was no question of my getting a grip on the particular company before I interviewed with them. It was also privately held, so I didn't have access to an annual report. It was the industry itself and my personal experience that I was selling. I knew I couldn't know the inner workings of a company like this anywhere near as well as the president with whom I talked did. All I could do was familiarize myself with general trends. They couldn't expect more."

Know when you are selling generic skills. One woman who made the move from the public to the private sector a few years ago also found there was little she could do to bone up on the specific company. She commented: "Basically, I was interviewing with generic skills, since I had management training skills that could be applied to any of several industries. There weren't a lot of times when I was expected to show off what I knew about a company or industry. I did enough homework to use some key expressions and terms. I learned that if you let people talk, and you listen, they like to tell you who they are. And if you just pick up the clues as to who they think they are, that can be as important as reading a financial statement." Only rarely, though, will you go on an interview where no real preparation is required.

Realize the limitations of homework. As noted earlier, most of the time you will use only a small percentage of what you know in an interview, and you'll be more impressive if you have all the questions in your mind rather than written down. There is really no point to filling your head with small facts, minutiae, and lots of figures. Doing so, in fact, may only make you panic during the interview, or worse, try to show off what you do know just for the sake of showing off.

How to Establish and Achieve Your Goals for the Interview

All this is leading you in one direction: toward the day you walk into someone's office for an important interview and put your knowledge to good use. Your questions should serve three purposes. First, they should impress the interviewer with the fact that you have done your homework. Second, they should show that you have experience the company can use. Third, they should help you get valuable information you need about the company in order to decide whether or not you want to hand over the next five to ten years of your professional life to this company.

Bear in mind, as you prepare to ask some tough questions, that an interview isn't a team sport. True, you are being interviewed to determine whether or not you're the right candidate to join the team, but at the moment of the interview, the only team you should be concerned with is you, yourself. Janet Tweed aptly noted the position of a job candidate when she said: "You are the only one who is going to be interested in you in this job. If you are outstanding in a job, it's because you are happy, well-paid, and, most important, you are in an atmosphere that allows you to function."

Because of this, you must ask some tough questions that allow you to determine whether you will, indeed, be happy, well-paid, and in an atmosphere that will allow you to function. Tweed commented: "You should ask tough questions. You should say, 'I read your annual report and it looks to me as if you had a bad year. How will this affect your people? I know you're having some problems with product identification. How is this division doing?'"

Can You Play Hardball During an Interview?

There are two schools of thought about how tough your questions can be. One holds that the very toughest questions can come only from candidates who have been recommended through an executive recruiter, who are thus presumably happily ensconced in their present jobs, and who have no intention of changing unless forces more powerful than themselves somehow make them an offer they can't refuse. In other words, the fact that you are in a position of being wooed gives you carte blanche to be the tough guy who wants to know everything because you must truly be persuaded to take this job.

Carrying this theory to its natural conclusion, this would mean that if you came to the company, as most job candidates do, in response to an advertisement or through a contact of your own and without the recommendation of a headhunter, then presumably you would not have as much freedom in your questions. And if you are currently unemployed or under pressure from your present employer to seek work elsewhere, then you can hardly ask tough questions. But Al Duarte thinks someone who is "looking" for a job should try to hang just as tough as someone who is being "recruited" for a job. He recommends: "Even if you're out of work and looking for a job, you should be as tough with a prospective employer as you can be, because if you make a mistake at this stage, you could ruin a whole career."

Duarte says, if at all possible, even an out-of-work executive should prepare to put some tough questions to prospective employers. "The candidate has to put the interviewer under some stress, too. He can say, 'You want me to consider your company, but your last year's results were not very good. Why?' Or 'You came out with five new products, and three were bombs. Why?' The candidate has to do this," Duarte said, "in order to evaluate the situation. Finding a job involves so much more than whether you like each other. If anything, the candidate's questions should be tougher than the prospective employer's questions."

He admits, however, that the very toughest questions can come only from an executive who is being pursued for the job. "Someone being recruited can even say, 'I wouldn't touch your company with a ten-foot pole,' and then let the company sell itself to him. It's the difference, again, of course, between looking for a job and being recruited."

Things to Think About When the Ball Is in Your Court

More than anything else, a job candidate's questions should be designed to determine whether the company is in trouble. The following warning signals should alert you to a company that may be having serious problems:

- no long-term planning
- morale problems
- lack of unity
- high turnover
- not enough turnover, making the company too inbred and leaving too little room for growth
- no new products when some are needed
- no clearly defined culture

- inflexibility in dealing with the marketplace; inability to respond quickly to customers
- too wedded to a rulebook to be truly creative or even responsive to employees' needs

Playing Your Best Shots

While many of your questions genuinely will be intended to gather information about a company, some will be designed to show off your expertise, experience, and intelligence. These are the kinds of questions that require the most probing pre-interview research.

Make your questions as comprehensive as possible. For example, don't simply ask, "How do you think the market for your product is changing," but rather, phrase the question this way: "Industry experts have been predicting that cable TV will take over more and more of the industry. Do you agree? If you do, how do you think the public stations can compensate?" This alternate line of questioning shows that you are aware of industry trends and forecasts and that you have given them some serious thought.

Other questions, though, can be even more pointed about showing off your knowledge and experience. For example, suppose you are interviewing with a software manufacturer and your pre-interview research uncovers the fact that the company just recently branched out into business software after years of exclusively supplying the game market. There has been talk in the trade press regarding problems with developing this new market. Phrase your question this way to make it comprehensive: "I understand you've had some problems building a market. Was this due to delivery problems or problems with quality control?" The real point to this question, of course, is that you have experience—and some intelligent opinions—about delivery problems and quality control. You have just managed to highlight your areas of experience and have invited further discussion about them. You have also demonstrated that you've done your homework and that you know something about this particular company.

Ask questions that go beyond the kinds of opinions and data you can glean from reading the business press. Show that you have taken the information you uncovered and digested it. In formulating your questions, ask yourself how the things you have learned apply to the division or department for which you are interviewing. Ask yourself what inferences you can make based on your reading, what problems you foresee. Then shape those thoughts into a question. The question format is best because you can avoid simply stating what you know and looking as if you are showing off. You are, but it's got to be subtle.

Word your questions so they cannot be misconstrued as an attempt on your part to give advice or recommendations to the company. This is never appropriate during an interview, unless you are specifically asked for advice, and even then, you should tread lightly, since you are still an outsider who may not—cannot—be privy to all the information you need to analyze a situation. The purpose of the questions is to initiate discussion during which you can show off your knowledge and the homework you have done regarding this company.

THE THIRTY-FOUR MOST IMPORTANT QUESTIONS TO ASK ON AN EXECUTIVE INTERVIEW

The outcome of your pre-interview research should be that you can walk into your interview with a mental list of questions that you're prepared to ask. The questions you actually ask will depend in large part upon whom and what you encounter during the interview. Following are two lists of potentially good questions.

Tough Questions You Should Always Ask

1. What are the most important responsibilities of the job?
2. What are other responsibilities?
3. What are the company's major long-term plans for the future?
4. Are you planning any major changes in direction?
5. What is the typical career path of employees?
6. Do you promote from within? (Then find out what's the best route to the top, that is, do people come up through sales or marketing or whatever department you are interviewing for?)
7. What is the turnover rate? (Pay special attention to whether people are leaving across the board, whether only top management is leaving, or whether only people in a certain function or department are leaving.)
8. Why is this position open?
9. Are you planning any new products (expanding into any new markets)?
10. Would you describe my areas of responsibility on this job? What job functions will I be responsible for?
11. What kind of staff will I have? What are their strengths and weaknesses?
12. What qualities did the person who held this job before me have?
13. What is the biggest negative about this job?

14. What is the biggest positive about this job?
15. Where can I expect to be next year?
16. What major changes in management or organization are you expecting in the next two years?
17. What exactly would you like me to accomplish in this job in two years?
18. To whom will I report?
19. How accessible will this person be to me? How will we work together, i.e., will he or she advise, have veto power, consult, permit me a fair amount of independence?
20. What budget is available to me, and what are the limitations on how I may use it?

As you read the Even Tougher Questions list that follows, you will see that many of these questions are simply tougher versions of the questions that appeared on the Tough Questions list.

Even Tougher Questions

21. Why wasn't there someone in the department who could be promoted to this job?
22. Who on my staff will resent me or cause problems for any reason?
23. I understand you're having some morale problems. How are you handling them?
24. The turnover rate is extraordinarily high. What's going on?
25. The turnover rate has been pretty low for about eight years now. Don't you worry about becoming stagnant? What are you doing to keep new ideas flowing?

26. What is the average tenure of employees who have filled my position?

27. I understand your acquisition of XYZ Company last year wasn't as successful as you had hoped. What are you doing on that front?

28. Why did that product bomb?

29. Why haven't you marketed this product more aggressively?

30. Why haven't you gone after this market?

31. Why didn't you change that marketing (or advertising) strategy when you saw it wasn't working?

32. Your profits have been low for the last three quarters. What are your plans to do something about this? Are you planning any layoffs?

33. You're known as a tough manager, particularly with your senior line executives. I like to work somewhat independently. Do you think we can accommodate each other in this area?

34. How will my performance be evaluated? More specifically, how will it be evaluated in the year or two that will be required before my efforts will have an effect on sales or productivity?

Finally, don't get so carried away asking about problems that you fail to discuss the good things about the company. For example, you might say, "I understand from reading *The Wall Street Journal* that your sales have climbed by thirty percent in just the last six months. How did you do that?" Or you might ask about a new acquisition: "I see that you purchased Elwood Foods. Are you planning to expand into foods, or was there something else behind this move?"

After an interview in which you have asked a lot of hardball questions, it is especially important to end the interview on an optimistic and positive note.

SIX

Basic Tools: Resumes and Cover Letters

Most people believe a resume will help them get a job. Most people are completely wrong. A resume can help you get an interview, but no one ever got a job, especially an executive job, on the strength of a resume alone.

If you are an executive, you have probably passed Resume Writing 101. What you may need to brush up on, however, is Executive Resume Writing 1001. It's true that the basic rules of resume writing are the same whether you're a secretary or a CEO, but there are still a couple of tricks you can use to increase the effectiveness of your resume.

Write several resumes, if necessary. The higher up the ladder you climb, the more specialized the requirements of a job. So the more important the job is to you, the more you should think about writing a "customized" resume, one that is specifically geared to the job you want.

Let's say you hope to fill the position of "division manager" for an old, well-established manufacturing company. Suddenly, Proctor & Gamble has an opening. You've already got a resume that describes your general potential prowess as a division manager, so isn't that enough? No. Let's say that one job ago you worked for a competitor and reported to a very creative division manager; furthermore, the person to whom you would report at

P&G is a tennis addict, and you have represented your company in organizing tournaments for junior players for several years. You definitely need to rewrite your resume to include these two very specific pieces of information because they may have some bearing on whether or not you will get this job. It's definitely worth the time and effort and the Sunday afternoon that will be required.

Don't use a professional resume-writing service. Of course, you can afford one—the best, in fact. And yes, the better services write solid, professional resumes. But many employers and all executive recruiters can spot one of these resumes a mile away. And they just don't reveal some very basic things about you—such as whether you can write a coherent sentence or spell "executive." Your resume is, in a way, the very first sample of your work that a prospective employer will see, and it should be *your* work and no one else's. *Exception:* Some executive-recruiting firms routinely recast job candidates' resumes into their own format. It's not a good practice, for the same reason that using a professional resume-writing service isn't, but if you want to work with this headhunter, you'll let him do this. Don't even waste your time protesting. In fact, if you protest, you may be seen as controlling or too detail-oriented.

Think twice about including a job objective on an executive resume. It's a mistake because you may write an objective that is too narrow and thus take yourself out of the running for another job, or you may write one that is too general and thus convey that you're in the market for anything you can get, or worse, not a very goal-oriented person.

The biggest reason, though, to skip the objective is that most people write very poor ones. They describe what they hope the company or job will do for them, when, in fact, a good job objective should describe what you could do for the company. Ned Klumpf commented that the typical resume objective reads like this: "I'm seeking a challenging position that will use my best abilities." It might better read, he says, like this: "I'm looking for an opportunity where my contributions will better the organization so that I will be able to contribute to my maximum ability." But since this is the kind of thing you want to emphasize during an interview, anyway, why not just wait and discuss your job objectives in person?

Pray there are no gaps in your career. Few things pop out more than a resume that accounts for October 1968 through January 1973, and then shows a gap of several months when you were obviously unemployed, picking up again in August 1973. Cover the ones you can (a year off to write a book, time taken by military duty, a year of graduate study), and ignore the gap you can't explain. Maybe the interviewer won't notice, but the chances that the gap won't be spotted are slight, so this is something you must be prepared to discuss and explain during an interview.

Finally, the Golden Rule of resume writing for executives is this: The heavier and more detailed (read: accomplishment-filled) the top part of your resume is, the lighter the bottom part should be. This means that if you have already held executive positions, and you've got nothing to apologize for or even explain when it comes to your experience, then you can drop a lot of excess baggage that you may have been carrying around since you wrote your first post-college resume. When you're seeking a senior vice-president's position in a bank, and you've already been a bank vice-president for eight years, then you don't need to describe what your extracurricular activities were in college. Just write the name of the college, the dates of attendance, and any academic honors. Similarly, just list professional organizations and affiliations unless you were an officer or organized something so important that it might help you get a job.

The Executive Resume

No one ever has much leeway in the format of a resume, but an executive has even less. You're too far up the ladder to use anything gimmicky; and the creative resume is definitely not for you. If a resume delivered in a film can got you your first break in the movie industry, now that you're in the executive ranks, don't even think about a replay. You should write a resume that is absolutely straightforward, particularly in its format. In brief, here's what your resume should look like:

- Use white paper. Any other color, including beige or gray, will look dirty if it's photocopied.
- Use black printing. It still looks black and strong if photocopies are made of your resume.
- Buy the best paper you can afford, a good bond, if at all possible.
- Print your resume on 8½-by-11-inch paper.

It's okay to make photocopies of your resume or even to use an instant printer—most of the time. You can even send a copy of your resume to a company that is looking for a CEO, *but* a specially typed resume will have that customized look that was discussed earlier. As a rule of thumb, if the job really matters, send an original, customized resume.

The Design of Your Resume

Give some thought to the look of your resume. Use orderly subheads. The first level of subheads might be all capital letters; the second level might be capital letters and lowercase letters underlined. Be sure to use the same subhead level for parallel chunks of copy. For example, if you use capital letters to announce "Employment History," then also use capitals to head

"Education." Don't, however, use a lot of fancy or different fonts. An executive resume should not be typed in italic or any kind of script copy, nor should there be very many capital letters or boldface heads. They're distracting to the eye and messy looking. Less is more, when writing an executive resume.

Make sure all the type on the resume is identical. Don't use your letterhead stationery for your resume. Type out your name and address and telephone numbers using whatever machine you will use to type the rest of your resume. Don't mix several kinds of type.

Leave a one-inch border all around the resume. White space creates an aura of neatness and logic.

Whether discussing your employment or your education, always begin with your most recent experience and work your way backward.

Keep the format consistent throughout the resume. If you use a paragraph format in one section, use it throughout. Use indentations consistently. Make lists consistent, especially in their grammatical forms. For example, in one list (or in all the lists on any one resume), don't write, "Ran company division" and "Supervision of staff of 80." Instead, write: "Ran company division" and "Supervised staff of 80."

The Length of Your Resume

Let it end naturally. An executive resume can easily run more than one page (although one-pagers are favored these days), assuming that your accomplishments warrant the extra page. Never pad your experience and accomplishments simply to stretch a resume to two pages, though, and never let a resume go on to a third page. The latter is far too professorial for the business world. If only one or two lines of a resume run over to a second page, cut a line or two and fit it all on one page.

Resume-Speak

Just as every business has its own jargon, so, too, do resumes have their own language. Resumes are often written without the use of the personal pronoun "I." If you decide to drop it, then do this consistently throughout the resume. Resumes should be written in a kind of literate shorthand, which you can quickly pick up from reading a few good samples. Use buzz words, a sample of which follows, to describe your achievements.

EXECUTIVE RESUME BUZZ WORDS*
data gathering of new product concept
product development
conceptualizing and implementing
create regional planning program
direct and manage large-scale programs
increasing profits (or product line or market)
increasing sales
decreasing costs in marketing, production
    and/or distribution
developing responses to government regulation
developing new decision process
identifying and correcting deficiencies in the process

Even more important than using buzz words, though, is to be sure to describe your responsibilities in dollars, if at all possible. Talk about annual sales, the dollar volume of projects you've worked on, the dollar value of acquisitions you participated in. Money talks—and never more than when you're trying to talk someone into hiring you for a managerial and administrative job.

----

* Thomas L. Weck, *Moving Up Quickly: How to Use Executive Job-Hunting Techniques to Land a Better Job* (New York: John Wiley & Sons, 1979), p. 82.

The Contents of an Executive Resume

Most executive resumes contain the following categories of information:

- Heading—name, address and telephone. Use your home address and give your office telephone number in addition to your home number, if you wish. Be sure to label each telephone number "home" and "office."
- A job objective or title (highly optional, as previous discussion made clear).
- Employment history, also called "Experience" and "Work History."
- Education, going back no earlier than college and including any graduate work, seminars, and special training that is career related.
- Publications. Unless you're looking for a job as a college teacher, don't go on at great length even if you've published extensively. When the publications list threatens to take over your resume, simply state, "Numerous articles published in ABC magazines and XYZ journals," and list no more than five to six of the more prestigious publications.
- Languages. List any languages you read or write. Never exaggerate your level of fluency.
- Military experience. Never skip this; it's too good a topic of small talk in the first few minutes of an interview.
- Professional affiliations. Personal information, such as your private club memberships, religion, and marital status are not included on resumes today, nor are they legal subjects of discussion during the interview. Professional affiliations, particularly if they may help build rapport, should be included.

- Statement regarding references. The names of references should never be listed on a resume, but never omit the statement that references are available upon request.

Resume Killers

Here's a list of things that consign your resume to the revolving file.

- any creative gestures or gimmicks
- any misspellings
- serious grammatical errors
- photographs
- handwritten addenda
- colored paper or fancy type
- poor copy of the resume
- onion skin paper or paper that is easily smeared
- vagueness
- puffery or obvious exaggeration of your experience
- unrealistic salary expectations (Never list your salary requirements on a resume, even if an ad you are answering requests this information.)

THE EXECUTIVE COVER LETTER

Send a cover letter with every resume you mail. Not to enclose one is a sign that you don't know the finer points of job hunting. It is also a missed opportunity to market yourself.

Write a cover letter on your own business letterhead. Never use personal stationery for job hunting. Like your resume, business stationery should be white with black type. Preferably, it should be 8½-by-11 inches or slightly smaller and of similar or the same stock as your resume is printed on. If the paper stock of your stationery is different, it should be on superior stock to your resume; never write a cover letter on stock that is inferior to the paper you have used to print your resume. Your business stationery should be the best bond paper you can afford, and it should be printed with a simple three- or four-line identification: your name, address, city and state, and your telephone numbers. Don't use any logos or mottoes. Choose a typeface that is clean and straightforward—and very businesslike. At this stage of job hunting, you want to fit in, not stand out from the crowd.

A cover letter should be written in business letter format. Start with a heading (your imprint), and follow with the date, inside address, greeting, body, close, signature, and typed name, in this order.

Even if your secretary typed the letter for you, her or his initials should not appear at the bottom, as is customary with your business correspondence. Neither of you is doing this on behalf of your present company. Nor should any job-hunting correspondence ever be typed on your present employer's letterhead; that announces to prospective employers that you don't mind pilfering from the boss.

If someone has requested your resume, enclose it with a short, typewritten note reminding them of this fact. If you are sending a resume on your own initiative, then the cover letter should contain the following information:

1. A statement describing your interest in working for the company.
2. The reason that you want to work for the company or the reason that you are sending them this resume.
3. A brief highlight from among your many qualifications,

particularly one that you know or believe is relevant to this job.

4. A request for an interview. Say that you'll call within a week to ten days to set up an appointment.

Although the last item on this list may seem redundant (Why else are you sending a resume except that you hope to obtain an interview?), asking for an interview is like closing a sale. Any good salesperson knows that you have to ask someone to buy something directly, and that if you don't ask, you may lose the sale. It's not enough to simply show a prospective buyer the product. If you don't ask for a meeting in your cover letter, your resume may be filed away—or even thrown away.

A resume and cover letter are relatively minor steps in the interview process, but they are the first impression some employers have of you. As job-hunting tools, they must be done right to do anything for you.

SEVEN

Psyching Out
the Interviewer

The success of any executive interview depends upon your abil
ity to psych out the person interviewing you. And your ability to
handle the person interviewing you depends on your having a
clear understanding of the power relationship that exists when
you, a powerful executive, are interviewed by another powerful
executive.

POWER VOLLEYING: THE THEORY OF POWER IN
AN EXECUTIVE INTERVIEW

**Remember that the power goes back and forth throughout an
interview.** A good executive interview is like a good game of
tennis. When the ball is in your court, you hold the power to
shape the direction of the game. When the ball is in your competitor's court, he or she has the power to shape the game. But
the important thing to remember is that the ball—or in the case
of the interview, the power—does go back and forth, first to one
court and then to the other. This means that each person has
opportunities to assume control.

There are times, of course, when the power balance is off

during an executive interview, and the interview begins to take on the air of a typical boss-subordinate relationship. Sometimes, you can't do anything to save a situation like this, but most of the time you can take some steps to equalize the balance of power. The kinds of things you need to do—and sometimes must do—are described in the pages that follow.

The balance of power is subtle. And you have a lot to do with keeping it delicately balanced. You should, for example, go into the meeting assuming that this is an interview between two peers. You can do some things that a subordinate can't. This means using first names. It may mean that you open the conversation. It may mean commenting on something—a painting or poster—in the office.

Don't overdo this, however, in an attempt to be friendly. Presuming a personal relationship where none exists, a popular technique of inexperienced or inept interviewers, is the wrong way to show off power. Resist commenting on anything personal, a photo or some memento on the desk, or something the interviewer is wearing. Especially don't comment on anything that indicates a school or club tie unless you want to let the interviewer know that you also belonged to the same school or club. Few initial conversations fall flatter than ones in which the job candidate enthusiastically says, "Oh, I see that you belonged to the Red and the Black." Glad to have a handle with which to start this interview, the interviewer, equally enthusiastic, responds, "Oh, did you belong, too?" Answer: "No."

Another way to maintain equal power is to get the person interviewing you out from behind his desk. Michael Korda in his book *Power!* understood the power of the desk. He also suggested that the powerful and the would-be powerful saw a few inches off the legs of office chairs so that anyone coming into their offices who sat down to talk would find themselves sitting several inches lower than the person behind the desk. But this isn't necessary. Simply being the person behind the desk gives one lots of power. So, if at all possible, suggest that the two of you sit comfortably around a small table or on a sofa or occasional chairs as you get to know each other.

Most of the things that maintain the power balance between you and the interviewer will happen naturally. If they don't, then you should take the initiative.

Whenever two high-powered managers are in the same room, even for an interview where everyone is presumably on his or her best behavior, the balance of power, always a very delicate matter, becomes even trickier to handle. While you want enough power to demonstrate that you are a take-charge person, you don't want to exert so much power that you threaten the person doing the interviewing. And taking control definitely does not mean being aggressive. According to Robert Hecht, the problem with executives is rarely one of not exerting enough control. He said, "Executives by and large are not a particularly passive or laid-back group. If anything, they err in the opposite direction. They become incredible or hard to take during an interview."

You must show the person interviewing you that you know where the lines of power are drawn. One employer interviewed for this book commented: "As the president of a company, when I interview someone for a vice-president's position, I expect to find out whether I can take his job and draw a pencil mark around it. I tell him I expect him to make it a big circle—as long as he doesn't start stomping on my toes or giving me fits or making me have to run behind him and repair a lot of damage. I want someone to whom I can delegate work, but I don't want a powermonger."

Your job, as an executive who wants a job, then, is to show that you have power, but that it is—and can be—controlled. You never want to appear so powerful that you are a threat to the person interviewing you, since he or she will usually become your boss if you are hired.

Consultant Ned Klumpf thinks that a person should be aware of whether or not he or she is so powerful that potential employers will be threatened. If you suspect you are the superaggressive type, then take steps to tone down your message. One way to show that you understand the limits to the job is to ask exactly what functions and areas of responsibility you'll be accountable for if you take the job. Then describe only those achievements that are relevant to those areas. Keep referring to the fact that these are your areas of *responsibility*. Try not to use the words "authority" and "power," as they can make you seem too aggressive.

A job candidate who knows he may be too aggressive, according to Klumpf, should be particularly careful when asked about long-term goals. Explain these goals carefully, alluding to the fact that you want to contribute at a higher level, but don't say anything direct about how you want to expand your "authority." An ultra-aggressive job candidate should never tell an interviewer he wants his or her job in five years.

On the other hand, Klumpf said, an executive shouldn't back off from power. After all, it's one of the qualities you have to sell. "A hiring executive wants to see some element of power in an executive he is considering hiring. What the candidate has to test carefully is how much power the interviewer wants to see. It all goes back to homework. If you've done it, you know how much power you can show. Some executives don't want anyone usurping their power. They are power managers. You must know the management style before going into an interview, or you can end up dead in the water."

THE FOUR BASIC INTERVIEWER PERSONALITIES

Most interviewers can be psyched out during the course of an interview. Bob Hecht says to do this you need to understand the personality style of your interviewer and then pattern your response accordingly. Hecht believes that most interviewers can be typecast into one of four different types.

Forecaster. This type of interviewer has one or two key questions, and based on your answers to those questions, he makes a forecast about your personality. Once he has done that, not much you say will change his opinion of you. To pass his test, you must be able to spot the meaningful questions, and, of course, you must answer them in a way that suits him.

Unfortunately, his questions are often psychological even when his training isn't. Typical ones are: "Where do you want to be in five years?" "What are your major weaknesses and strengths?" "What do you consider to be the major accomplishment of your career so far?" Sometimes they aren't psychological, but they're still designed to test you. He may present a work problem and ask you how you would handle it. Listen to his questions carefully so you can shape your answers accordingly. If his questions are philosophical in tone, give him an answer that has philosophical overtones. If they're action-oriented, make sure your answer is, too.

Associator. The Associator wants above all else to hire someone who fits in well, who matches the company's and his own personal chemistry. A team player, in other words. And team players, to him, anyway, are people with whom he can associate certain familiar things, such as you both having graduated from the University of Michigan or your mutual love of tennis or golf.

To impress this interviewer you must reach out and help him see the associational ties that will make him comfortable with you.

Systemizer. The Systemizer is the toughest interviewer to get past, because his criteria are based on sound, logical thinking. He needs proof of your qualifications and evidence that you can do the job before he will hire you.

To impress a Systemizer, you must carefully present your case, emphasizing the achievements and strengths that make you right for this job. He is hard to get past, but eminently fair.

Energizer. Unfortunately, there are more of these around than any other kind of interviewer, although their numbers are diminishing as executives learn skilled interviewing techniques. The Energizer makes an intuitive decision in the first few minutes of the interview about whether or not you are right for the job. For him to be impressed, he needs to sense that you both have the same kind of energy.

An Energizer isn't all bad if you can make a good enough impression to be one of the anointed ones. But this type of interviewer also has a serious drawback, most notably that you and he never settle down to a serious, in-depth conversation about the job. He never really gets to know you or finds out whether you are truly qualified, and you are so busy impressing him that you don't find out if the job is really right for you, either. Unfortunately, this only sets things up to fall apart later—six months or a year into the job, for example. There's not a lot you can do to handle an Energizer except hope that the energy is right.

How to Respond
to the Interviewer's Personality

Once you have figured out which personality type you are dealing with, the interview will go more smoothly and you will have a surer grip on the direction it is likely to take. Understanding the kind of person you're dealing with also means you can respond appropriately to his personality type. Bob Hecht advises, "In posing your answers, try to talk the same language as the interviewer. If, on the one hand, somebody talks to you about concepts, the ideas behind what you have done, then you should describe the concepts on which your actions were based. It's wrong to say to that kind of interviewer, 'The hell with the concepts. Let's talk about the results, and I'll tell you something about the process.' If you do this, you've missed the cue. The interviewer may, in fact, be interested in results, but he will still be uncomfortable with the fact that you're not talking his language.

"On the other hand, if someone says to you during an interview, 'I don't care what your thinking was or how you justified your actions, just tell me what you did and how long it took you and whether you can do it again,' then you skip the abstractions and logic behind your actions. If you insist on spending three hours on the concepts and underlying logic of your achievements, this person won't see you as his kind of person, either."

In addition to appraising the interviewer's personality, it's important to understand how the interviewer feels about interviewing and hiring other executives.

The interviewer is under some stress, too. Although it may come as a surprise to you, he or she is as scared, if not more scared, than you are. After all, here he is interviewing someone for a $50,000-plus job, and if he doesn't bring in the right person, or the person he brings in doesn't work out, the blame will fall on him. He will have cost his company a lot of money. He can easily make a poor call if he is not careful here. In addition, hiring isn't something he does everyday, and he may be well aware that he lacks even the most basic skills he needs to make a wise choice.

The fact that an interviewer is under so much pressure explains a lot about many interviews—the directions they take, the awkward silences, even the awkward conversations. An important part of psyching out an interviewer is to measure his or her stress level and then do whatever you can to put him or her at ease and to make the interview go more smoothly.

HELPING THE INTERVIEWER INTERVIEW YOU

Not every interviewer you encounter will know how to conduct a thoroughly professional interview, and one of the things you must take into account when you take stock of an interviewer is how skilled he or she is. Even when an interviewer is skilled, you will have to know what's happening, what his techniques and methods are, in order to make the best of the interview.

HOW TO HELP THE UNSKILLED INTERVIEWER

Human resources people are generally quite skilled at interviewing executives on any level, but line executives don't fare so well. After all, they usually haven't taken any courses on interviewing techniques; they don't interview job candidates very often; and they don't really know how to go about conducting an executive interview. As a result, if the interview is to go well enough for you to become a viable candidate for the job, you will have to help the inexperienced or unskilled interviewer interview you. To do this, you must know when you are being interviewed by someone who is inexperienced.

Six Signs of an Inexperienced Interviewer

1. **Inexperienced interviewers give too little thought to planning an interview.** One of the key things an executive should do before an interview is write down the interview questions, yet most executives don't. Instead, they tend to ask whatever comes

into their minds, and at most, they have three or four general questions they always ask. Depending upon the answers they get to those questions, they then let the interview take its own course, however meandering and irrelevant that may be. When you encounter a situation like this, you have no choice but to take control.

2. Inexperienced interviewers tend to play amateur psychiatrist. And this is a major mistake. "Too often," according to William Byham, president of Development Dimensions International, a training and development firm, "the interviewer asks questions such as, 'Tell me three good things about yourself or three bad things' or 'Tell me what kind of father you had.' In doing this, the interviewer manages only to project his own values and needs on the job candidate, and besides, most executives make pretty poor psychiatrists. The more they try to be psychiatrists, the more they make bad hiring decisions."

From a job candidate's point of view, it is often painfully easy to see through such questions and give the interviewer the answer he wants. Interviewers who ask about your father, for example, want to hear about your heroes, they want to know that you had heroes, and they may even vie for the job if they become your boss.

The smart way to deal with this question and other questions like this from these office-chair psychiatrists, is to tell them what they want to hear. Unfortunately, this does not always bode well for the course of the interview. Sometimes, you can gently steer an interviewer to a more realistic course, but often the interviewer doesn't progress past the point of idealistic exchanges that reveal little of what either participant needs to know.

3. Inexperienced interviewers often have an unclear picture of what is required to do a job. Every management consultant interviewed for this book echoed the statement of one who said, "I frequently work with two or three managers interested in filling a position. When I ask them what they're looking for, I get

three entirely different answers—even though it's the same job."
One executive admitted the difficulty in defining certain kinds
of managerial positions when he said, "The more general the
job of managing, the harder it is to make a decision about
whom to hire, and the more often the decision is based on
impressions. It's only when you break down a job and are specific about what you are looking for that you can get past man-
nerisms and personality traits."

Whenever a prospective employer doesn't have a clear picture
of a job, it's easy enough to sell yourself to him or her. The
only problem is whether you want such an ill-defined job. It's
better to try to pin down the person and see if you can get him
to describe the job. If he simply cannot describe the job (and
this isn't as rare a situation as it ought to be), you should probably treat the interview (in your mind anyway) as a throwaway.
You can't accomplish a job that can't be described.

**4. Inexperienced interviewers tend to ask single-edged ques-
tions.** These are questions such as "Do you like your present
job?" or "Do you enjoy managing large numbers of people?"
that can be answered with a yes or a no. In this situation, help
the interviewer by elaborating a little when answering.

**5. Inexperienced interviewers don't give the interview the
importance it deserves.** They permit interruptions; they don't
turn off the phone. An effective interview requires 100 percent
concentration on the part of both parties. It should be private.
Outside interference should be kept to an absolute minimum.

Unfortunately, there's nothing you can do if an executive in-
sists on taking phone calls during an interview. You should,
however, take this as a very bad sign. Either this executive
doesn't think you are important enough to warrant his full, undivided attention or he isn't a person who is capable of giving
his undivided attention to anyone or anything. Do you want
this person for a boss?

6. Inexperienced interviewers place too much importance on intuitive and snap judgments. They mostly subscribe to the theory that a relationship is made—or not made—in the first four or five minutes of a meeting. "If you don't do well in the first few minutes of an interview with these people, you've struck out," says Bob Hecht.

First impressions aren't always right, though, particularly in situations where the next five to ten years of your life are at stake. Executives who rely heavily on their intuition often fall prey to the halo effect, a recognized interview phenomenon.

When the halo effect takes over, according to William Byham, this is what happens: "The interviewer jumps too quickly to a decision. He has a few words with a job applicant and then decides that this person is good or bad. That would be all right if he or she went on to test these assumptions. But that's not what happens. What really happens is that the interviewer selectively gathers additional data that supports the original assumption. If he already decided that the person was pretty good, then the questions that are asked will reinforce this assumption. Even when an interviewer gets data that operates against his original decision, he tends to discount it. Even worse, when this kind of interviewer decides that someone is bad or not right for a job, then he doesn't even hear the good things that might come later in the interview."

One research experiment showed the strength the halo effect has on people. It consisted of a videotape of a job applicant describing his qualifications for a particular job. He had excellent qualifications, but there was one major negative reason that he wasn't right for the job. The videotape was edited in two ways: in one version, the negative came out at the beginning of the interview; in the other version it came out at the end of the interview.

The videotape was shown to executive recruiters who were

asked to indicate if they would invite the candidate back for a second interview. Most of the recruiters who got the negative information early in the videotape nixed the person for a second interview. And most of the persons who heard the positive information first passed on the candidate for a second interview. This experiment was especially interesting in that all the interviewers heard exactly the same information about the person being interviewed. That's how strong the halo effect is when it is in operation.

Sometimes the halo effect works in reverse, as when an interviewer makes a snap judgment that he or she doesn't like you. One recent job hunter recalled, "I certainly went on interviews where the person had either made up his mind the second he looked at me or was totally distracted or just didn't like my tie. The interview was a joke. It's clear enough quick enough when this happens." And there is little you can do to counteract that kind of snap judgment—in much the same way that there is little damage you can do to yourself once the halo effect has gone into operation in your favor.

HOW TO HANDLE THE SKILLED INTERVIEWER

Skilled interviewers, in contrast to unskilled ones, present another sort of problem. They are often very good at interviewing and can pose a genuine threat if you don't understand what they are all about. A good interviewer is one who has had training in conducting interviews. His questions are probing, in-depth, concrete, and you will have to learn how to handle them in order to avoid making a serious error that will take you out of the running for a job. You may even have to use some self-defense to make sure you don't get trapped into making a ruinous error. Not that a skilled interviewer will try to trap you.

Quite the opposite. He won't even subject you to any unnecessary stress if he can help it. But his questions and his interviewing techniques may be so skilled that you find yourself saying things you didn't mean to say, telling him more than you meant to tell him—in short, putting your foot in your mouth in a big way.

Six Signs of an Experienced Interviewer

1. **Experienced interviewers lay out the job.** They tell you what they are looking for up front. The interviewer may not begin by describing the job, but at some point during the interview, he will describe the culture of the company, the kind of department you'll be responsible for, the areas of responsibility, and the functions of the job. He will go through your background with you to see if there's a good fit.

2. **Experienced interviewers ask double-edged questions.** These are questions that cannot be answered with a simple yes or no. Examples of this kind of question are:

Tell me what you especially enjoy about your present job?
What was the biggest problem you've encountered in your
    present job?
What do you think will be the major obstacle in this job if
    you decide to take it?
What would you consider to be the elements of your back-
    ground that have most prepared you to handle this job?

3. **Experienced interviewers get you to say more than you intend to say.** Mostly, this occurs through the use of restatement and reinterpretation. In the former instance, he will restate what you have said: "So you think there aren't any drawbacks to taking this job. Is that correct?" Then he'll wait for

your answer, and you will usually blurt out some drawback that weighs heavily on your mind but that you hadn't thought appropriate to discuss with him. The truth is that you should discuss *any* drawbacks to the job with your prospective employer, but the way to do it is with planning and forethought, not by getting caught unawares in a way that makes you bare your subconscious thoughts in a disorganized way.

A good interviewer also may attempt to interpret something you have said: "You lost that job because you challenged the boss, but you think that was an unusually difficult boss?" Again, an appeal has been made to your subconscious. You have given your prepared answer, but now you're being asked the same question in a slightly different way. The answer is, "Yes, I've given that a lot of thought, and I think that was indeed the situation." What's more likely to come tumbling out of your mouth is something like this: "Well, actually, I have had some trouble with authority in my past and I think in some ways I rebelled against my boss inappropriately." Needless to say, this information has no place during an executive-level interview.

4. Experienced interviewers act empathic. By acting empathic, the interviewer is testing you, and he's trying to get you to reveal a prejudice or weakness. The police use empathy to get criminals to confess; good interviewers know this works equally well during job interviews. The interviewer will give you lots of empathy in order to make you say things that will put you in a bad light. For example: "I understand things have been pretty rough over there." You open up and tell him just how rough things are on your present job, and he decides you are a disloyal crybaby. "I've been out of work, and I know how it feels." One job candidate broke down and started crying when an interviewer said this to him. Even the toughest person will unload too much if he's not aware of what is going on.

Equally destructive is the sympathetic nod. You tell a sexist joke or make a slightly racist remark (just to test the waters, you tell yourself) or talk about politics or the economy. (You would be surprised how often comments like this will come tumbling out of your mouth at the wrong time, or maybe you think it is the right time since you've heard how conservative this interviewer's politics are.) You get a sympathetic nod, so you continue. What you don't know is that you have just hung yourself. Even if the interviewer or the company is known for its political alignments, and you have spouted the right party line, the subject was inappropriate for an interview. And you lose.

The interview will be friendly enough but short. You will never hear from the interviewer again. The nod was a ploy, something that was used to get you to put your foot in your mouth. It worked. Unfortunately, no one looks like executive material with his foot in his mouth.

5. Experienced interviewers use compliments to get you talking. People melt a little when they are complimented even by their worst enemy, and when a compliment comes from a prospective boss, well, it has a tendency to make one a little more talkative, to make one open up a little more.

Don't succumb to this; simply smile and say thank you when a compliment comes your way.

6. Experienced interviewers ask disarming questions. This is similar to all the other techniques—in fact, all these techniques are similar in that the interviewer tries to win your confidence so that you will talk more openly with him than you might otherwise or than you should. To disarm you, an interviewer will tell a short story about a mistake he's made, and then ask or imply that you have probably done something equally silly. The next thing you know you are describing something very silly that you did—something so silly that the interviewer realizes he doesn't want to hire you.

The Advantages and Disadvantages
of a Good Interviewer

Good interviewers are skilled, and you can get a good, fair interview from one. But you can also fall into a lot of traps if you aren't savvy enough to spot his techniques and counter them if need be. You shouldn't be dishonest with these interviewers; just don't let them talk you into saying more than you should. Particularly beware of camaraderie that develops during an interview. You aren't on the same team yet.

HOW TO TAKE CONTROL
WHEN THE NEED ARISES

Sometimes an interviewer is so inept that the interview will go nowhere unless you take control. Keep in mind, though, that it is always risky for a job candidate to seize total over of an interview. It's risky because all interviewers think they're good, even if they're not. Al Duarte described the major danger of a job candidate taking this bold step: "It's tricky to take control from a poor interviewer. If you try to do this, you may consciously or unconsciously antagonize the person behind the desk."

Bob Hecht disagrees, however, and feels that if a candidate knows how to be interviewed, he or she can probably, without letting on, control the interview and thereby get the interviewer to do a better job of interviewing. Hecht describes the technique of taking control from an interviewer in this way: "The job candidate plants directions, ideas, or pathways of discussion that are designed to uncover the qualities and qualifications of the applicant without the interviewer recognizing that he is being led rather than responded to. I call this anti-interviewer training.

"For instance," Hecht went on to say, "an inexperienced and

probably poor operating manager might say, as they so often do, to a candidate, 'Tell me about yourself.' Now that's an open-ended question to which a candidate may reply in any way that he or she sees fit. It's like a blank slate; you just fill it in any way you want. If the interviewer had in mind that the answer would tell him how important the candidate's perceptions are of what's important to him, that's one thing. But if the interviewer wants to hear something specific, he may not hear it unless the candidate takes some control. When a broad, open-ended question is asked, a sharp or trained interviewee will ask a couple of questions to help the interviewer focus on exactly what he or she wants to hear."

Sometimes, an interview goes so poorly that you must assume even more control. Janet Tweed described a situation where an interviewee might really have to take over an interview: "Let's say we're talking about a plant manager position, and the person doing the interviewing is the vice-president of manufacturing. This man is interested in manufacturing the product, getting the raw materials, and getting the product out on time with low waste. He might need a plant manager tomorrow, but he's not an interviewer.

"Shortly into the interview, the job candidate should realize that the interviewer is not asking the right questions to elicit his background. The candidate can wait a fair amount of time and then say, 'Look, as a plant manager at ABC Manufacturing, I'm proud to say that I was able to reduce waste by thirty percent.' He should then go on to a small monologue describing his achievements. And then he should shut up."

"In using these interviewing techniques," Hecht noted, "the interviewee gently—and not so gently at times—guides the interviewer into specifying what he is interested in by showing him that the broad gauge is not so useful as the short gauge."

Five Ways to Stay on Top of an Interview

Other ways to stay on top of an interview are:

1. **Always know where the interview is headed.** Be aware of where the interviewer is leading you. Ask yourself what kinds of things he is trying to learn about you. Is this interviewer going to lean heavily on your past experience, or is he going to be more impressed with qualifications from your present job? Does he want to review your past positions or hear only about the job you now hold? Does he want to see how you can conceptualize, or is he interested in hearing facts and figures?

2. **Always be alert to inferred meanings.** You spend a relatively short amount of time in any interview, especially when you consider how much of your future life depends on its outcome, and it's easy for misperceptions to crop up. Listen for these and do what you can to adjust or erase them.

3. **Always be alert to any biases on the interviewer's part.** If you are an attractive woman, for example, and you sense that an interviewer may not be taking you as seriously as he or she might because, you presume, the interviewer thinks all pretty women are bubbleheads, then you would want to avoid any small talk or irrelevant chatter during the interview and concentrate on putting forth your heaviest qualifications for the job.

Another common bias exists against single people. Beyond a certain age, a single man has always been suspect in the job market, and increasingly today, single women are suspect, too. Much of the suspicion that surrounds single men is simply jealousy over the assumption that they have freewheeling lifestyles. If they aren't encumbered by a family, then employers fear they won't have any reason to be serious workers. To counteract this prejudice, a single man may have to make a comment or two noting that his life is not all play and little work.

Kathryn Stechert, an expert on women and work, believes that single women are beginning to be discriminated against, too. They are viewed either as a distraction or grind. If a single woman is attractive, then prospective employers think she will be busy looking for a husband. If she is not so attractive—and sometimes even when she is—a single woman may be viewed as someone who will work harder than her married colleagues because she doesn't have any family responsibilities.

Both biases must be corrected during an interview, if possible. In the former instance, a woman can act very businesslike and be sure her most serious qualifications are brought out during the interview. In the latter instance, she may have to remind the interviewer that she enjoys vacations, sports, and other assorted activities that take place outside the office—in her leisure time.

Finally, you should realize that the interviewer may have biases you simply cannot overcome. His biases may constantly cause him to make decisions that are bad—such as not hiring you. Unfortunately, interviews with people like this are often throwaways, and you can't do much with them.

4. Always be responsive during an interview. Don't plan what you're going to say next while the interviewer is talking. It always shows on your face. To show attention, say "Hmm" or "yes" occasionally. Leaning forward in your seat is another way to show that you are paying attention to what is being said.

5. Learn to recognize when you are losing the interviewer's attention. Actually, an interviewer does you a favor when he sends overt signals that you are boring him or say something that lets you know you have lost his attention. "You've lost the interviewer if he cuts you off or interrupts you because you're going on too long or if he asks you a question that he just asked you a minute ago or one that is a non sequitur," according to Hecht. "You know he's not paying attention because you just answered that question two questions ago.

"If you see this happening, it's best to let the subject go and get onto something that evokes a positive response. Give control back to the interviewer and let him redirect the interview. You can say, 'Well, look, I've said enough about that. If you like, we can get back to it later. What other things would you like me to talk about? What's important to you? I want to use your time productively, so you tell me what you want to know.' This way, you give him back control, but in essence, you have remained in control, too."

How to Establish Rapport

Regardless of how well you are able to control an interview or manipulate an interviewer, or whether he is good or bad, there is one aspect of the interview that you can't control very much, and that is the establishment of rapport. Rapport is what happens between you and the interviewer to make you feel you have an affinity to one another. It may consist of finding out that you both grew up in the same part of the country, that you both love jazz, or that you both started your careers with the same company. A sense of rapport puts both of you at ease, but it also helps to build intimacy, an even more important purpose.

Once an interviewer feels a sense of rapport with you, he or she will also feel comfortable asking you questions that check out your values and ethics—questions, for example, about your views on family life, the economy, women's rights, as well as questions about what you really want out of this job or why you don't like your present job. You should be prepared for this, and should also realize that you can trade on your rapport with him or her to find out more about the company and the interviewer's attitudes and views. Usually, rapport is established fairly early during an interview or not at all.

The interviewer is the one who attempts to establish rapport. Robert Hecht pointed out, "It is the interviewer's job to do this. It is up to the job candidate, though, to know what to do with an opening to establish rapport. If the interviewer gives you an opening to talk for a minute or so about last night's football game, and you choose to hold forth for twenty minutes on the merits of the two teams, then you have not used the chance to establish rapport well. The interviewer will think there is something wrong with you, that you don't know what you're there for." Don't miss an opportunity to establish rapport, but don't abuse it, either.

The best small talk is related to the job or the interview. Don't flinch when the interviewer asks you something mundane, such as "Did you have trouble getting here" or "How was the food on the plane?" He is trying to put you at ease, and if you both are comfortable discussing something this minor, you will have an easier time moving on to the more important things you have to discuss.

Try to be aware of when the small talk is ending. Generally, it's up to the interviewer to end it, just as he started it, but be sure you let him do this. Keep your answers and comments brief, and at the appropriate moment, stop the banter and be quiet. That's when the interview will begin in earnest.

KNOWING WHERE THE POWER ULTIMATELY LIES

All the psychologizing about an interviewer and all the anti-interviewer techniques in the world won't do you much good unless you keep in mind who really holds the power during the interview process. It's true that you are equals; it's true that you can gently wrest some control from an interviewer and help him or her get a better interview; but the overriding truth is that the interviewer has the power to hire you—or not, as the case may be. That power ultimately lies with him or her. As a result, you must recognize there are limits to how much control you can exert during an interview. You cannot be too aggressive. You cannot threaten the interviewer. You must demonstrate that you understand the limits to your power. If you don't do these things, you won't get hired. It's that simple. And you can't make an interviewer hire you because you're the best candidate for a job if he or she doesn't like you as a person or doesn't find you credible as an executive.

It is also important to know when to let go of interviewers who can't be won over. That way, you can concentrate your time and energy on interviewers and interviews where the chemistry is right.

EIGHT

Basic Questions You Have to Answer During an Interview

Interviews consist of questions. If you aren't asked many questions during an interview, the interview is in trouble.

There is something of an art to answering the kinds of questions you will be asked during a job interview. And the questions only become more probing and tougher the higher up the ladder you go. A high-power executive job never comes easy.

Perhaps the biggest decision you must make during an important interview is how closely to shape your answers to the interviewer's questions.

Project what is required to get the job and shape your response accordingly. There is a big difference between projecting what you think the interviewer wants to hear and projecting what you think the job requires. In the former instance, you may bend any experience or qualification to make yourself look qualified. In the latter instance, you will use your experience and qualifications to show how they would enable you to perform well on the job.

THE EIGHT CARDINAL RULES OF ANSWERING INTERVIEW QUESTIONS

Here are eight basic rules that will get you through even the toughest questioning:

1. Keep it brief. Don't talk too long. This is perhaps the most common sin of executives when they interview. When you're the boss, you can discourse at will and length. During a job interview, you can't—or rather, you shouldn't. You won't be very appealing if you turn your prospective employer into a captive audience.

Try for three- to four-sentence answers. If you must give an answer longer than that, divide it into parts by saying: "There are three reasons for that."

Make a special attempt to keep your answers short during the first few minutes of an interview before you've had a chance to check out the direction of the interview and the interviewer's personal style.

2. Stop talking when you've said enough. Even if the interviewer sits there in silence after you have given an answer, don't start talking again. Lots of people hang themselves because they can't stand a little silence.

The interviewer could be using the silence deliberately to make you uneasy enough to say something more—possibly something you will regret. Or he could be mulling over what you've said, which is probably a good sign.

3. Listen carefully. If you do this, you will find that interviewers tell you a lot about themselves and a lot about the company. You can use this information to impress the interviewer during the interview with your grasp of the company and the position.

Pay attention, too, to the content of the interviewer's questions. Does he ask about how your authority has expanded over the past few years, or is he more interested in how you have been limited? If he asks about the latter, he may be letting you know that he runs this show and that your powers under him will always be somewhat limited.

Another reason to listen carefully is that you'll appear inept if you misinterpret a question. Imagine expecting to be asked one thing and actually being asked—and responding to—another. Never hesitate to ask for clarification of a question, if necessary.

Listening well means listening actively. Use your whole body and your facial expressions to listen. If you are planning what to say next, it will show in your face. Lean forward slightly in your chair. Nod in agreement. Look directly at the person interviewing you.

4. Don't be modest. You are there to sell yourself, and sell yourself you must. Describe your achievements and don't hesitate to mention ones you aren't asked about directly. Some key phrases will help you describe your achievements without sounding overly boastful. For example, say such things as, "I'm especially proud that I managed to . . ." or "I think that was the achievement that meant the most to me personally." Another way to harp gently on your achievements is to rate them: "That was a minor achievement, but one that I'm proud of nonetheless." "Yes, I think that was my major accomplishment on the job." "Of the things that I accomplished, there are two I'm especially proud of."

5. Don't exaggerate. Don't say you did something you didn't do. Don't say you played a more important role in a project than you did or that you did something alone when in fact you had considerable help in masterminding it—or weren't even the mastermind at all. John Foster said, from a recruiter's point of view, that he will disqualify someone who exaggerates on-the-job experience: "Often, I'll find out after the interview that the person didn't really do all the things he said he did, or that he certainly didn't do them by himself. He took the credit and someone else did it, or he shared responsibility with someone else."

The CEO at a Fortune 500 company noted, "People have a tendency to overemphasize their experience. It's awfully easy to check with references or find out from the person during the interview whether he really had the decision-making responsibility he claims to have had. If a job candidate goes in trying to make too big a case, and that means any kind of distortion about the responsibilities you had, you're dead in the water as far as I'm concerned."

6. Talk in concrete terms. There are two ways to do this: First, through the use of examples that describe your work experience, and second, through the use of numbers that show how you measured up on your present or on past jobs. Examples and numbers are proof that you get results, be they products, sales, or some other criteria, and results are one of the things that will most interest a prospective employer. They show that you, as a manager, have a growth record, and that you know and understand the industry.

7. Never defend or argue a view during an interview. Why? For the very simple reason that you can't win. You may be right, in fact, but you will also appear defensive, and that's a fast way not to get hired.

Bob Hecht explained why this is never a winning technique: "If the interviewee tries to wrestle power by intimidation rather than explanation and persuasion and justification, then you have two battling machines who are defending each other against one another. Nobody wins an argument in an interview, least of all the candidate. This is because if you're going to start out arguing, the prospective employer will conclude that you're going to be a tough cookie to live with, and who in the hell wants you around?"

8. Make connections for the interviewer. It is vital that your experience and qualifications be connected to the requirements of the job for which you are interviewing. If the employer is using an executive recruiter, the job will have been clearly defined at the start of the search, but whenever you go into an interview through some other contact, one of the first things you will have to ascertain is how well defined this job is.

If the prospective employer does not have a clear picture of the job, it is up to you to make the kinds of connections that will enable the interviewer to see you as the best qualified candidate of the job. One way of viewing this situation is to realize that the person interviewing you has a problem or set of problems to solve. These are the requirements of the job. You can help him solve the problems if you can figure out what they are.

You can ask directly what the requirements are for the job. If the interviewer cannot give you a straight answer, then you may have to get at the requirements in some other way, usually by giving him choices about what he wants to hear about you. If he asks a question about your present job experience, for example, you can respond by saying, "My job responsibilities fell into three areas: sales, management, and marketing. Which of the three are you most interested in hearing about or would you like to hear about first?" His answer will give you a clue to the requirements of the job. If he wants to hear about sales, then sales experience is probably something he is looking for in the person he hires.

TWENTY-TWO QUESTIONS YOU SHOULD BE PREPARED TO ANSWER

Most of the questions you'll be asked in an interview are predictable. Each question is important, and you should have a good idea of how you plan to answer these questions before you go into an interview. Here are the ones you will hear repeatedly:

1. **Where do you want to be in five years?** Everybody is wise to this question, but it still gets asked, mostly by unskilled interviewers. Job candidates hate it because it puts them on the spot. Often, in fact, you want the job of the person interviewing you. And just as often, people who ask this question are threatened if you say you want their job. In addition, saying you want the job of the person sitting in front of you has, in the words of one recruiter, "gotten to be too clichéd—like motherhood and apple pie."

Experts disagree over the best way to answer this question. One job-hunting veteran said, "It's particularly difficult to answer the question without saying you want the boss's job. If you show that you are very ambitious, which is what they think they want to hear, then the person interviewing you often feels personally threatened. He thinks you won't stay on the job more than a year. If you give a wishy-washy answer, he may be happier, but you may be seen as a rather indecisive person."

One employer noted, "It's not my chair that someone wants to be sitting in, anyway. It's my chair at some other company. I think a person is pat and naive when he or she says he wants *my* job."

A recruiter warns, "In some cases if you don't tell the interviewer you want his job, he'll wonder why you want to work for him. It depends on the level of the person who is interviewing you. Sometimes you can say, 'I want your job. But I can see that you're obviously going on to bigger and better things.'"

A management consultant says it is always a risk to tell the boss you want his job: "I would never tell anyone I wanted his job in five years. I used to say that, and I used to think it worked, but I was working at lower levels in management. As I got higher up in corporations, I thought it was the wrong answer, mostly because it was too big a gamble. The odds are too great that you're going to tell it to the wrong person. I'll only gamble when the odds are fifty-fifty, and when you go up the corporate ladder, I think the odds are only seventy-five–twenty-five. There's only one chance in four that the person you say this to won't be threatened."

So what is the best way to answer this question? Look at its real content, for a start. What you are really being asked is to show that you think in terms of the future, that you set your goals five or ten years down the road. Talk about what motivates you, especially what will motivate you on this job. Do you need to be challenged constantly? Does money motivate you? Does power motivate you? Without saying you want the boss's job (there seem to be more reasons not to say this than to say it), describe where you would like to be in your career in five years, as well as what you hope to have accomplished.

2. Why are you leaving your present job? The correct answer to this is that you want better opportunities for advancement or more responsibility, or both. If you are changing careers, you might also add that you want to be in an industry that is going to grow more than the one you are presently in. It's not a good idea to use money as a reason; besides, it's obvious that you will want more money. That's a subject for another conversation.

3. Tell me about your personal interests. The interviewer who asks this may be trying to find out several things about you: whether you're a workaholic who has no outside interests; whether you're so devoted to outside interests that they may interfere with this job if you take it; how much drive and ambition you have; and how intellectually inclined you are. Most employers these days want healthy, well-rounded executives, so don't say you have no personal interests and that you live only for your job. Exception: The one time that this might be the right response is when you are clearly sitting across from a workaholic who is looking for a clone.

Otherwise, try to give a qualified, honest, and middle-of-the-road answer. Mention a favorite sport that you participate in; and if it seems appropriate for this job or this interviewer, mention that you also like to use your leisure time to read. But don't sound so passionate about an outside interest that it threatens to be more important than your work.

4. What are some of your more rewarding personal achievements? Like the question that preceeds it, this question is an attempt to find out what kind of person you are, that is, what really makes you tick. The best answer is an honest one, so long as it puts you in a good light. You might say that you paid for your own college education, did some charitable work outside the office, earned an advanced degree, or, especially these days (for men *and* women), manage to combine parenting with a career.

5. Why should I hire you? The interviewer who asks you this is really probing four qualities: (1) your readiness for the job, (2) your ability to handle it, (3) your willingness to work hard at it, and (4) your fitness for the job. As for your readiness, describe how your career path has prepared you for this job. To show off your ability, point to specific skills and accomplishments that demonstrate you can do the job. Talking about your motivation or attitude, even your assertiveness, will show your willingness to do a particular job. As for your fitness for the job, a prospective employer wants to hear that you are able to get along well with other people, that you are reliable, and that you are flexible enough to handle the challenges that will come with this job.

6. From whom have you learned the most during your career? Usually, this question comes from company heroes or from people who work in companies with hero-oriented cultures. The interviewer wants to know who your heroes are because he or she thinks they will reveal who you are. Appropriate answers are a former or present boss, a much admired professor, or a parent or some other role model who taught you a lot about business and/or encouraged your career.

7. What gives you the most satisfaction during your leisure time? This question is similar but not exactly like the question asking you to describe your personal interests. If you have not yet been asked about your personal interests or leisure activities, now is the time to describe them briefly. Then tell—honestly— which ones give you the most pleasure. If the answer doesn't tie in with the kind of work you do, then it should in some way show how well-rounded you are as a human being.

8. How do you set priorities on your time? This question probes how well organized you are. And depending upon who is doing the asking, it may be a query about how important your career is vis-à-vis your family and vice versa. If you sense that the question is only about your time at work, then respond by saying, "I like to have my day fairly well-organized, but I always leave some time for emergencies. And I think any schedule must be flexible enough to accommodate the unexpected occurrences that always come along."

If you sense that the question is about your family versus your career, then another answer is required. Ten or fifteen years ago, an executive was someone who knew that his work came before his family because his work was what sustained his family. He never admitted to loving his family or putting them first during a job interview if he really wanted the job. All that, fortunately, has changed. Today, many companies admire a person who frankly states that his family is the most important thing in the world to him (or her), and that they come first. Other companies, while not anti-family, like their executives to value both, and it's more appropriate to respond with something like this: "The two most important things in the world to me are my family and my career. I try to divide my time so that I can pay the necessary amounts of attention to both." To know which kind of company you're interviewing with, you need to know something about the company's culture.

9. What would you like to have accomplished in your present job that you haven't? This is the kind of question asked only by a skilled interviewer. There is no hidden message or meaning in it; the interviewer is simply probing to see how analytical you are. Your answer should show that you are reflective, that you review your actions and attempt to learn from them. Of course, if you are in one of those rare jobs where you have managed to accomplish everything you set out to do, then you should state that—and go on to say that's why you're ready to move on to bigger challenges.

10. What would be the toughest (most enjoyable, least enjoyable) aspect of this job should you take it? This is another way of getting at your strengths and weaknesses, but this question is also usually asked only by a skilled interviewer, so it is also an opportunity for you to discuss any reservations or minor apprehensions you may have about the job.

11. What problems do you think the company faces over the next year? Five years? This is an attempt to see how analytical you are, and to see how perceptive you are about this particular company. This is a trick question to the extent that you must answer what you are asked, which is to say, you should describe only the problems you foresee. Don't offer any solutions, unless specifically asked to do so, and then do so only with greatest caution. You can't possibly know as much about the company as insiders do, and you are in far too vulnerable a position to offer advice on running the company since you're still an outsider.

12. How would you deal with a subordinate who resents your presence? What you are really being asked is how you wield power. Your answer should show that you wield it judiciously, and you should also take note that some problem employees may come along with this job. In fact, you may want to ask some follow-up questions once you have answered this question so you can explore the problem more fully.

Probably the best answer is one that indicates that you will review the employee's background and record, that you will talk with the employee to try to ease the problem, and, finally, that you will eventually fire the employee, if necessary. Mentioning the fact that you would release an employee if things can't be worked out is an important and necessary step since it shows that you can assume the necessary authority to manage people.

13. How would you handle stepping into a department that was set up and run for many years by one well-liked and well-respected person? Again, judicious behavior on your part is called for. And measured authority. You should indicate that you would show respect for the elements of the organization that work well for you, and certainly wouldn't reorganize a department just to do things your way, but that there may be some things you will need and want to change because they will suit your organizational methods and management style.

14. How will you handle a department with a morale problem or a poor record in other ways? This is a straightforward question that calls for a straightforward answer. But if this is the kind of operation you will be taking over, this is something you should have uncovered during your pre-interview research. That way, you can present a well-thought-out answer.

Before answering this question, you also need to know whether you are being hired as a turnaround person, that is, as someone who will clean up an ailing operation and put it back into working order. Turnaround people are tough and fast-moving. They don't usually stay on once they've cleaned everything up, since long-term, stable management is not one of their specialties. If you are a turnaround person, your answer will be tougher than if you are being hired for the long term. You can be more forthright about the way that you will clean house if necessary.

If you are not a turnaround person, your answer will be more temperate and analytical. You might compare this situation to one you were in or observed someone in; you should talk about the positive things you will do to improve morale and build up people's motivation, and you should probably indicate, depending upon the company's culture, that you would fire only if necessary.

15. What are your goals on your present job for the next few years if you were to stay on there? Careful, this is a trick question, albeit a fair one. If you describe a lot of unfinished work on your present job, you may reveal an attachment to it that will raise some questions about how serious you are about changing jobs. The best answer goes something like this: "I think that I have basically accomplished what I set out to do when I took the job," or "Given the restrictions [the limited budget, the management problems], I feel I've accomplished as much as I can on the job and that I'm ready to move on to other challenges."

16. How can you contribute to solving this company's problems if you are hired? Careful, again, this could become a trick question if you do not understand what you are being asked. You are not being given carte blanche to tell the interviewer how you would run the company unless you are being interviewed for the position of CEO, in which case that's exactly what you do.

Emphasize your strengths and qualifications, drawing on specific examples from your experience, to answer this question. For example, you might say, "Most of the problems have centered around the new product line, which as I understand it, has not performed up to your expectations. When I worked at ABC Company, I had experience on three different occasions in introducing new products, and I think I could be a major contributor of ideas on getting better performance out of these products."

17. We expect your division, should you take this job, to grow substantially in the coming year. What kind of plans for growth do you foresee? You will want your plans for growth to match those of the person interviewing you, i.e., the company, as closely as possible. This is where your homework can pay big dividends. You should go into any interview, after a proper amount of watching industry trends, armed with a plan for how you would strengthen or bolster or otherwise positively change your areas of responsibility. Here's your chance to use your background reading to make a forecast for the future.

18. What factors are most important to you in ensuring your satisfaction on this job? This is an easy one. Just tell the interviewer what it will take to keep you happy on the job. Warning: You aren't being asked to name your price yet or to discuss perks. This question is more about job satisfactions such as room to expand, new challenges, large budget, freedom to make your own management decisions than it is about dollars and company cars.

19. We think you should hire a good person right under you, and this would involve creating a new position. What would you look for in such a person? Be sure you describe the kind of person who would really fit this job, although the description will vary depending upon the position you are applying for. You aren't describing just another subordinate but, rather, a right-hand person who will work closely with you. Try to give some kind of concrete description in answer to this question, but hedge your bets by noting that you would probably have to get some hands-on experience for a few months before you would know exactly what kind of person you would most need.

20. Which of these job responsibilities appeals to you the most? The least? This question, which often comes toward the end of an interview or at least toward the end of the discussion about the requirements for the job, is basically something of a test to see whether you understand what's important about this job.

Describe the responsibility that you, based on your conversation with the interviewer, think is the one you would most enjoy. Say there are no parts of the job that you will not enjoy, that it all sounds interesting to you.

21. How does your family feel about this change? The answer should be that your family feels great about it, although you can be honest and admit to any minor problems, such as, "My teenage daughter isn't too thrilled, but she's moved before, and she'll be a real trooper should we move again." This is also an opportunity to bring up any family-related problems, which usually means a spouse's career. If there are real problems, be sure to discuss them, while indicating at the same time that your family is supportive of your career.

22. How is your search going? This question makes many people feel insecure, but it shouldn't; it's a perfect opportunity to let a prospective employer know that he has a little competition. The right answer to this question will show that you are indeed looking around, and that you are conducting a thorough, well-organized job search. Basically, you should say that you are talking to the competition, or you may also want to say that you're exploring the same position in several industries. Either answer will make you look desirable. Be sure, however, that you do know who the competition is. The interviewer may ask if you've talked to such-and-such a company yet—usually an important rival—in an attempt to test how seriously you are looking around.

NINE

Blockbuster Questions

Almost all interviewers and executive recruiters have some questions in their repertoires that are quite literally interview-breakers. If you don't answer one of these questions correctly, there is little you can do after that to save the interview. A skilled interviewer will ask the blockbuster question and then pursue it until he is satisfied with the answer—whether or not he likes what he heard. An unskilled interviewer, however, is harsher and will immediately rule you out if you don't pass his blockbuster test.

Blockbuster questions are usually threatening. This happens not because the interviewer is trying to threaten you or deliberately subject you to stress but because the questions put you on the spot. A typical blockbuster may ask you to point out a weakness in yourself. The element of threat in this question is obvious. Not to answer it directly is to ignore the content of the question; to point out a serious personal defect is to put the job you want in jeopardy.

THE SIX MOST FREQUENTLY ASKED BLOCKBUSTERS

Some blockbusters get asked over and over again. You would be a rare job candidate indeed if you didn't run across at least one of these in every interview. Here are the questions and some suggestions for answering them:

1. Tell me something about yourself. This is the most obvious question in the world, but it is nonetheless a standard interview question, and you can often forget the rest of the interview if you don't come up with an acceptable answer. When it is asked, it is usually the first question in an interview.

First off, understand why this question is asked and the kind of answer you are not supposed to give. This question is usually asked out of anxiety, because the interviewer doesn't know any other way to start the interview. The purpose of the question is not to flatter you, and the interviewer does not want to hear your life story. Obviously, you know better than to answer with, "Well, I was born in . . .," but you would be surprised at the number of people who respond by saying, "Well, I attended college at . . ." That's an inappropriate answer, too.

If you're an executive, the only correct response is to describe your experience. And since you don't want to launch into a monologue at the outset of the interview, the best approach is to ask another question.

Ask the interviewer what he wants to hear about you. Would he prefer to hear about your early career, and even perhaps a little about your educational grounding, or would he prefer to hear about your most recent experiences and responsibilities in your present and next-to-last job? Let him choose, and then tell him the basics. Don't talk too long since the interview is just beginning. When you have said enough, shut up and let him make the next move.

2. Why do you want to work for us? This blockbuster is your best opportunity to impress a prospective employer, but few people are smart enough to use it this way. Most people take this question at face value and describe what they hope to gain from the job. That's the wrong approach to this question.

The person who asks this question doesn't really want to know why you want to work for this company; he or she wants to know what you can do for the company. The prospective employer wants to know what he will be getting if he hires you. According to Robert Hecht, "In return for the money and compensation package an employer offers, he will be expecting a return on his investment. He doesn't want to know what this job will do for you, that it will make you happy, or that it will give you a chance to be creative. He wants to know what the return on his investment will be. Will the company make more money, save money, or do something better or faster if they hire you? That's really what getting a job is all about. You hire someone because he'll do the job for you, more profitably, more efficiently, and faster than the other candidates you talked to."

3. Tell me about your past employers. This can be a trick question. The interviewer may well know that your present boss is an awful person to work for, and he may be testing to see how honestly you answer this question. So if your present boss is pretty widely known as intolerable, or if the two of you haven't gotten along, and this will possibly come out when your references are checked, then you must respond with an honest, but carefully planned, answer that still makes you look good.

Ned Klumpf says there is only one way to respond to this question: "As an interviewer, what I want to hear is how you solved the problem of having a tough boss. I don't want to hear what an SOB he was. If your boss was a real SOB, the smart thing to say is that he was a nasty man to deal with, but boy, did you ever learn from him. You learned that he was an excellent delegator, and he taught you some skills that are invaluable to you. Stress that you learned how to deal with a difficult person. Close by indicating that while you learned to cope with a problem boss, you now think the time has come to make other plans. Keep everything you say about a problem boss very upbeat."

4. What would you say are your biggest strengths and weaknesses? This is the dumbest blockbuster question, but it gets asked a lot. It's silly because no savvy interviewee is going to reveal a serious weakness about herself or himself—certainly not one serious enough to put the job in jeopardy. And what could be better than being asked to describe your strengths to someone whom you hope to impress?

If the question is two-part, always describe a weakness first and then end on a strong note—with your strength. In any response, try to tie in your description of a strength or weakness with the requirements for the job.

The trick to describing a weakness is to mention something that is actually a strength. For example, say: "I'm very tenacious. Once I start a project, whether it's training to run a marathon or untangling a problem at work, I don't let go until I've finished the job." What a weakness! What boss could ask for anything more?

There is also a way to play hardball with this question and admit to a real weakness that does have you worried. This opens the door for you and your prospective employer to discuss these weaknesses honestly. For example, one man was being interviewed for a vice-president's position for a larger corporation in the same industry. He was a project manager who was ready to graduate to being a person in charge of many project managers. When asked about a weakness, he was very up front about what he felt he would have to learn to handle the job. He said: "As a project manager I never had to learn to deal with what I think of as the boundaries. The vice-president I work for does all the fronting for the organization, and my job is to manage the project. If I take this job, I'm going to have to learn to do two things. First, I'm going to have to learn how to delegate authority to project managers, and second, I'm going to have to learn how to deal with a different audience from the one I've been dealing with."

Despite the fact that he had been very open and honest about describing his apprehensions over taking this job, he also had managed to present his weaknesses in such a way so they couldn't be used against him. He impressed the people interviewing him so much with his response that he got the job.

Make sure the strength you describe is directly related to the responsibilities of the job you hope to get. If possible, turn this into an opportunity to handle any doubts or misperceptions about you that may come up in later questioning. For example, if you know that you will be required to manage fifty people, and you have only been managing five people, you might shape your response this way: "I have most enjoyed managing other people. Although I've only been responsible for a few people's work, I consider this to have been a distinct advantage. I think I've learned much more about managing people from my small team than I would have learned from a large team, and now, of course, I'm eager to apply what I've learned to a larger staff. I've been able, for example, to develop some incentive and team techniques that I probably wouldn't have had time to develop had I been put in charge of a much larger group of people two years ago."

5. What do you like most about your present job? Find an answer that applies in some way to the job you're being interviewed for. If you have been working in new-product development, for example, and you want this job because it is also involved with new-product development, then say this. If you are being considered as a general manager, then an appropriate response is that you have enjoyed the varied responsibilities of your present job. Say you enjoy the unexpected challenges that come up every day, that you're happiest with a schedule and working style that is flexible, so you can accommodate the things that really need to be handled.

6. **What do you like least about your present job?** If possible, mention some function or area of responsibility that has nothing to do with the functions and responsibilities of the job you hope to get. And, of course, the answer should be framed to make you look good. For example: "For the last year, because of an unexpected change in staff, I've been carrying the marketing responsibilities. While I've learned a lot, and I'm sure I'll apply some of the things I have learned to my next job, and I'll always be grateful for the extra area of expertise, I have to admit I don't enjoy the marketing. Despite that, I think I can honestly say I've done a good job of handling this responsibility."

Note two things about this response: One, you have been careful to turn a negative into a positive by stating that you have learned something you will always be able to use, and two, you have made yourself look good by stating that you did a good job with this responsibility even though it wasn't your favorite responsibility.

FIVE OTHER HANG-TOUGH QUESTIONS

Depending upon your individual circumstances, here are five more tough, stressful questions you may encounter during an interview.

1. **Why were you fired?** This is the toughest question you will have to answer during a job interview. Your answer must have

substance; you can't gloss over something this important or respond in a way that fails to satisfy the person who is asking it.

Don't offer excuses. Acknowledge what has happened to you. Whether you were fired or officially laid off is of little consequence most of the time. If you insist you were laid off as opposed to being fired, a tough interviewer can come right back at you by asking an even tougher question: "You'd been with the company for five years. They laid off ten percent of the managerial staff. Why do you think you got laid off instead of someone who's still there?"

Try to give the real reason you were laid off without sounding as if you are making excuses and without making yourself look bad. For example, if you had a personality conflict with your boss or your style of management didn't match the company's style of management, discuss this without either putting yourself down or bad-mouthing your ex-employer. You might say of a company whose management style turned out not to match your own: "As you may recall, Tom Smith was CEO when I went to work for ABC, Inc. About two years later, he left—he was fired just as I was—and Ed Jones came in to run the company. While he did an excellent job, and I learned a great deal from him, from the beginning we didn't see eye to eye on how to manage a company. He wanted me to push my sales staff harder and cut incentives at the same time. I understand that he was brought in as a belt-tightener, and I agree that there was room to cut fat, but I don't think you start with your sales staff. I think they're the lifeblood of an organization. I guess I opposed him too vigorously. At least a year ago, I saw that we were never going to see eye to eye on management matters. I have nothing personal against him, and I think he would say the same thing about me—so I geared up to look for a job. It's a coincidence that they cut staff before I started to actively look for a job."

In giving this response, you have done several important things: First, you presented a concrete example of what was wrong. That will help your cause tremendously, much more than vague excuses ever will. Second, you described the source of the problem: new management and conflicting management styles. Third, you indicated that the differences were professional, not personal. This shows you do not have a personality problem and won't have interpersonal problems on your next job. Few employers want to take a chance on someone with ongoing personality problems, and getting fired always raises a red flag in this department. Fourth, you showed that you were doing something about—or learning something from—the challenge. In this case, the person said she was already looking for a job at the time she got fired because she was aware of the conflict. In other circumstances, you might say that you knew you had a difficult boss, but you still felt you were learning things, so you wanted to stay a little longer.

2. Why are you changing careers? This is a trick question. It is not so much that employers object to career changes as they want proof that you can handle a job in a new field. But—and here's what makes the question tricky—the way to convince someone is *not* to point out that there really aren't that many differences between the two fields, although this is often the case since management skills are management skills and can, in theory and in practice, be applied anywhere. One woman who had successfully changed careers and had at the same time moved from the public to the private sector, described the best way to respond: "I found that employers like you to list the similarities between the fields, but they also want you to recognize that they're different. In fact, if you stress that there won't be any difficulty, and say that you think the jobs will be pretty much the same, the person interviewing you often feels you aren't being realistic. You really have to tell the person you think this company is unique, and that although you think you will work very well in this culture, you also think there will be some adjustment involved."

Another person, a man who transferred from university administration to publishing, noted, "If you're making a career change, you have to explain why, and it has to be truthful, but you also have to be responsive to the person interviewing you. You have to make the change sound concrete and reasonable not just to yourself but also to someone who will want to hire you. You can't just say you had a vision in the night even if you did. You have to say something plausible to them—plausible, that is, from the employer's perspective."

If there will be some real problems in making the switch from one field to another, discuss them with the employer, but follow up by saying that you have always enjoyed learning new things and have always picked up new information quickly, and that you don't expect to have any problems doing so this time. Stress your flexibility and how much you enjoy and rise to a challenge. If possible, almost in passing, offer a concrete example, such as the time in college when you changed your major from eighteenth-century literature to astrophysics and still made the dean's list, or the summer you spent immersed in a completely new culture so you could master a new language.

3. Why have you changed jobs so often? This question makes most people feel somewhat defensive, although it shouldn't. Frequent job changes used to be a negative on someone's resume, but it's just not much of a problem today, as Janet Tweed pointed out: "There are certain industries where there is a lot of job-hopping. A person can have seven jobs in a career and nothing is thought of it. I'm not too concerned about the job-hopper if he gets in, gets good experience, realizes he's blocked because of one reason or another or is too channeled, and then moves onward and upward."

Tweed said that a series of brief job stints does sometimes raise a questioning eyebrow, but that it is one that can be explained away by describing what has happened and how you learned from your mistakes: "I think that my first job was problematic. I took the job right out of school, didn't look into the situation as carefully as I would now, jumped into it, and had to admit that I didn't use good judgment. When I realized that I wasn't the only one who was unhappy with the company, I took another job as quickly as I could. In a sense, I guess I fell into that job, too. But I realized early that it was wrong for me. Before changing, though, I did a lot of thinking, planning, and discussing, and today I'm quite clear about what I want."

4. Why are your earnings so low? This question is especially asked of women, who often confirm, when they go job hunting, what they have long suspected: They are being paid less than their male counterparts. Sometimes, the question is a surprise to a woman; more often, a woman knew all along that she was being paid less than the industry standard. Either way, according to Kathryn Steckert, her answer should be the same: "I think it's obvious that I'm underpaid, and that I'm worth far more. In fact, I expect to be paid up to my full value on my next job. I took lower salaries because they led to the jobs I wanted and enabled me to get experience I might not otherwise have gotten. I now feel, however, that I've done my work in the trenches, and I expect to be paid what I'm worth for my experience and expertise."

5. Why have you been looking for a job so long? Of course, how long you have been looking for a job is absolutely relative. To someone who has never been out of a job, two weeks of looking seems like too long. For someone who has been fired or laid off, six weeks seems like a reasonable amount of time, considering all the thinking, planning, and preparing that is required to set up a professional job search you weren't expecting to be involved in. Experts say an executive should anticipate being out of work one week for every $10,000 of his or her last salary. That means that an $80,000-a-year person will need a *minimum* of eight weeks to find a job, that someone earning $150,000 should brace himself or herself for a search of roughly fifteen weeks.

Now that this question has been put in perspective for you, you are ready to put it into perspective for the person who asks you about it. As with all tough questions, answer as honestly as possible while putting yourself in a good light: "I spent three weeks in planning and research. I wanted to be very certain of which direction I wanted to go this time, so I spent many hours in the local library and talking to various people about my future, as well as about my specific skills and talents. Since I started looking actively, I've been offered several jobs, but haven't found the one that is exactly what I'm looking for. While I'm eager to settle in somewhere, I'm not panicked and I don't want to jeopardize my career. I'm prepared to wait until I find the right job." An answer like this is beautiful because it turns what could have become a negative for you into a positive: you have taken so long to find a job because you're so valuable and such a good planner that you don't intend to make a mistake.

As you have probably observed by now, the toughest question about the touchiest areas of your career must always be turned around to your personal advantage. The trick to answering tough questions successfully is to respond in an upbeat, positive manner.

TEN

Projecting The Corporate Image

According to one experienced job hunter who has also for many years been an employer of executives: "It's probably unfortunate, it's certainly unfair, and it may be immoral, but first impressions are absolutely critical, especially in terms of your appearance. You make that good first impression, and then you can get down to technical abilities and experience. But if you don't make that good first impression, you may never have a chance to get down to anything."

Even before you shake hands with an interviewer, he or she is observing how you look and on some level—conscious or subconscious—will have found you either acceptable or wanting. If you were found wanting, it's hard to regain lost ground during the interview.

THE RIGHT STUFF

It's important to look like an achiever. And the good news is that most executives do. According to Al Duarte, most executives are quite savvy about their images: "I see very few executives who are overweight, poorly groomed, or who don't know how to dress. Most executives have an 'executive look' about them; that's part of how they got to be executives in the first place."

Here, then, is a brief refresher course, to be sure you're up-to-date on what's in and out in corporate dress. There are a few variations based on industry, a few more based on geography, but in a word, the way to dress for an interview is *conservative*.

The Choices If You're a Man

If you're a man, your choices are few. A good suit, a white shirt, black shoes, black socks, a dark, patterned or striped tie. The only real choice is what color suit, and that's not much of a choice. The acceptable—and more important, the safe—colors in suits for an executive are blues, dark pin-stripes, and gray. Gray is best worn during the spring and summer months.

And of these three suits, the very best one—the power choice—is the dark blue suit. Look in the closets of men who make the best-dressed lists; watch the power tycoons who surface in the television news; observe the suits of lawyers who handle the big cases; check out, in fact, any powerful, rich, well-dressed man and more often than not, he will be wearing a dark blue suit. It spells power.

It also spells flattery. It's a color that flatters every skin tone and body build. It makes paunchy men look trim, and trim men look positively sleek.

The suit should be three-piece. The white (or maybe light blue) shirt should be long-sleeved, with a crisp, unfrayed collar, either button-down or standard. Wear tie shoes, with plain toes or wingtips, if your business is very conservative, although in many businesses today, you can get away with less conservative shoes, even a good loafer. Your socks should be long. You can wear cufflinks, but they should be in good taste, certainly nothing unusual or flashy.

Your hair should be freshly cut, but for a haircut to look

good, it should be about one week old. If you have a heavy beard, and the interview is late in the day, shave again.

If you wear a coat, it should be a basic camel, navy, or black overcoat or a good trench coat.

The Choices If You're a Woman

A few years ago, John Malloy, author of the best-seller *Dress for Success*, set the world of business dress on its ear. Large numbers of women had just begun to reach the executive ranks and they weren't sure what to wear. Malloy solved their problem by giving them a uniform: the dress-for-success suit. The dress-for-success suit is a female (but not very feminine) version of the man's conservative business suit. It is two-piece, with a blazer and a flared skirt, tastefully hemmed to a length right below the knee. It is tailored of men's suiting fabric. With it is often worn a tie scarf—the one soft touch in the whole outfit. Shoes are black, navy, or a similarly neutral color. Basic pumps are the acceptable style. One lawyer said the uniform was so rigid in her profession that she couldn't wear shoes with straps; only basic pumps would do.

Many women, however, have chosen not to adopt the dress-for-success suit. It's a favorite with younger women in their twenties and thirties, and women in male-dominated professions such as certain old-line corporations and law firms, and in banking, but older women, particularly those who made it to the executive ranks before the dress-for-success suit came along, and women in more relaxed professions, primarily advertising and arts-related fields, often choose to wear a softer look. It consists primarily of Chanel-style or other softer-cut suits and silk dresses. The dresses are topped with a blazer or jacket of some kind.

Image experts have become increasingly disdainful of the dress-for-success uniform, arguing quite correctly that it isn't very creative. The small amount of research that has been done on the way executive women dress shows that women have far more leeway in their dress than they think they do. No one says the dress-for-success look doesn't work, but many women are finding out they don't have to wear it.

An interesting issue arose regarding Geraldine Ferraro's dress when she was campaigning for vice-president. Almost immediately the critics began carping that her style of dress wasn't businesslike, that she didn't wear the power uniform for women. One wise image consultant, though, pointed out that Geraldine Ferraro was naturally very powerful, and that her instinct to dress in a softer, more feminine way was right for her. She was using her dress to soften her highly assertive, powerful image.

The dress-for-success suit has served its purpose. It was invaluable for conveying a message about women's desire to be taken seriously at the time when women needed a way to send that message. But now that the message has been sent and received, professional women can safely branch out into other kinds of business dress, and some women can take a lesson from Ferraro.

Regardless of which look you choose, here are a few guidelines to help you dress for interviews.

Choose neutral colors, preferably beige, navy, camel, burgundy, gray, or brown. Some women can get away with red, but it's probably too flamboyant for most, and other hot colors such as orange, bright green, pink, and turquoise are not appropriate for a job interview.

If you wear a dress, add a jacket. A woman should wear an outfit whether or not she chooses to wear a dress-for-success suit.

A woman's purse and shoes should match or be complementary colors. Her briefcase, if she carries one, should not clash with the shoes and purse she wears.

Your shoes no longer need to be the basic pump, but they should be conservative. Boots are not appropriate for the executive suite, unless a blizzard strikes on the day of the interview. Even then, it's better to wear boots and change into shoes before the interview. Flats are sometimes acceptable; spike heels are not; a medium-height heel is always best. Sandals and slingback pumps are not considered very businesslike. Wear neutral-colored hose.

MAKEUP Makeup is a special problem for women since so many women use it to express their individuality. Although no one expects a woman to wear no makeup, most employers say they would eliminate a woman as a serious job candidate if she showed up wearing too much or the wrong kind of makeup. Unfortunately, what is considered too much or the wrong kind of makeup depends largely on individual taste. Women bosses are as likely to be put off by too much makeup as men are.

Blue or green eyeshadow headed most employers' unacceptable lists, followed by a too-heavy dose of blush. Excessive eyeliner also frequently met with disapproval.

There is no reason for a woman who wants to wear makeup and who thinks she looks better in it to avoid it, but makeup should be applied subtly. If a woman has any doubts about how she wears makeup, an image consultant who specializes in businesswomen should be consulted.

A woman should wear only a subtle or sporty perfume if she wears any at all during an interview. Even if your perfume is lovely, you won't want it to be a subject of discussion when you're trying to sell your qualifications and experience. And let's face it, throughout history perfume has been considered seductive. It's probably okay in the office—and it's probably too risky on an interview.

Keep jewelry to a minimum—a watch, gold or silver earrings, perhaps a pin or necklace. Avoid anything that jangles or glitters.

WHAT NOT TO WEAR ON A JOB INTERVIEW IF
YOU'RE A WOMAN

Several items of clothing and adornment are completely inappropriate for an executive interview. They are:

- Minidresses
- Unusually long dresses
- Ultra-high heels
- Gaudy jewelry
- Too much jewelry
- Heavy perfume
- Heavy makeup
- Large purses
- Pants
- Pantsuits
- Ultra-high fashion outfits (unless you're trying to get a job in fashion)
- Bright colors
- Prints

WHAT NOT TO WEAR ON A JOB INTERVIEW IF
YOU'RE A MAN

Some items of clothing just don't work for men in the executive interview. They are:

- Short-sleeved shirts
- Casual shoes or shoes that are any color but black
- Flashy cufflinks or jewelry
- A pinky ring
- Short socks (so leg shows when you sit down or cross your legs)
- Suspenders (they're okay once you're hired in some places, but it's better not to risk them on an interview)
- Bow ties (ditto above comments)
- Anything but the most conservative colors and patterns in ties

Hair—Still a Bugaboo for Many

The sixties may be long gone, but all those men who hated long hair or facial hair have only risen higher in the ranks of power, which means that the one area of grooming where people are still unreasonably opinionated is hair.

One hair expert conducted a survey of employers' tastes in hair color and styles, and here's what was discovered. According to the Leslie Blanchard Study of Executive Women, hair color is not an issue, but hairstyle is. Unacceptable styles on women include long hair (meaning anything longer than shoulder length), frizzy hairstyles, and hair that is excessively short. Mind you, once you get the job, the rules are a bit more lax, but if you know you're going to be interviewing any time in the next year, it's a good idea to begin to style your hair into an acceptable length and style.

In the eyes of most prospective employers, the most acceptable style for women is fairly straight or wavy, medium-length hair, with or without bangs. If bangs are worn, they shouldn't obscure the eyes.

One thing you don't want is a hairstyle you have to fiddle with. At least for the period when you're interviewing, avoid any hairstyle where you have to keep pushing your hair back off your face. You should avoid any hairstyle that requires a lot of maintenance to look impeccable.

Surprisingly, hair is even more of a problem for men than for women. Facial hair is the single trait that is most often mentioned by recruiters and prospective employers as being offensive and unacceptable. One recruiter reported, "I can call a client and tell him I've found a candidate who walks on water, but he's got a beard. Lots of clients will turn him down. So I tell my client, shave it off or skip the interview."

A career consultant noted, "Let's face it, everyone has pet

peeves. If a man is smart as a whip, a Harvard MBA, he's thirty-five, he's got ten solid years of experience, and he's got a center part with curly golden hair down to his collar and a mustache and a beard, lots of employers still won't like him. A candidate has to dress the part to play the game." And there you have it in a nutshell. Most of the time, in most industries, eccentric (in the eyes of the Establishment) hairstyles and facial hair have to go if you want to play ball with the big boys.

As important as whether or not you have a beard or a mustache is the style in which you wear your hair. Most executives don't wear outlandish haircuts, but not all executives recognize the importance of having a good barber. Find someone who knows how to cut your hair, and get regular haircuts. That way, you won't be in the situation of scheduling an important interview on short notice and finding yourself unable to get a badly needed haircut.

GROOMING: THE WAY YOU PULL IT ALL TOGETHER

The Leslie Blanchard Study of Executive Women also found out that prospective employers seek employees who are businesslike, hard-working, confident, and well-groomed. Most career experts interviewed for this book thought well-groomed should really top the list. It's part of your first appearance, and if you don't look neat and well-groomed at first glance, there's little chance you will be seriously considered for any job.

Grooming means immaculate, the opposite of sloppy. It goes without saying that there's no room for missing or loose buttons on a coat or suit, unshined shoes, rundown heels, unsewn hems or torn anything, dirty fingernails, unkempt hair, or unpressed clothes—even if you've traveled some distance to the interview.

Of this list, unpressed clothes is probably the item that causes the most trouble for some women, since linen is a popular fabric for summer suits. Frankly, you're better off not wearing linen for a job interview.

Of course, you may find that you have to work all day and go on to an interview at 5:30 or 6:00 PM, wearing the same clothes you put on nine hours earlier, which will inevitably look a little worn at this stage. Employers take this into account and won't hold this against you. What will hurt is wearing yesterday's wrinkles. There's an obvious difference between a suit that has wrinkled during the course of one day and one that has been worn two or three days in a row without pressing.

One man who was interviewing for a high position in a bank lost the job, after passing the first interview with flying colors, when he showed up for the second interview in the same suit. The interview had been set up on short notice and he had flown to Los Angeles from San Francisco expecting to return the same day. Instead he was invited to dinner, which ran late, and was then invited back the next day to meet some more people. Through no fault of his own, unfortunately, he ended up wearing the same suit two days in a row and was disqualified from the job because of it. The solution: Always be overprepared. If you travel out of town for a job interview, arrive early so you can go to your hotel room and change into fresh clothes for the interview. If something comes out of the suitcase wrinkled, call the hotel valet and get it pressed. Even if you think you will only be out of town for the day, or for overnight, take an extra day's clothes along so you're ready for the unexpected.

It should go without saying that the biggest part of grooming is cleanliness. Clean body, clean hair, and clean hands. Your hands should not only be clean but they should be well-manicured. Women can wear nail polish, so long as it is a pale pink or peach color; for men, in most businesses, clear nail polish is not acceptable. A bigger problem is bitten, chewed nails and cuticles. These are a sign that you are an anxious person, and that's a bad omen in the eyes of many employers. A surprising number say they check out the condition of a job candidate's hands.

If you have a chance, it's a good idea to wash your hands (and check your overall appearance) immediately before you go into an interview. Especially if you've read any newspapers, you may have to remove some newsprint, and if the interview is at the end of the day, the grime of city living may simply have built up to make your nails less immaculate than they might be.

INDUSTRY VARIATIONS IN DRESS

There are industry variations in how people dress for job interviews. Some companies, for example, are known to be image conscious, among them IBM and Bristol Meyers. So is the entire banking industry. Old-line companies, which range from banking establishments to law firms to manufacturing firms, are known to require conservative dress with a capital C. You *must* wear a dark blue or pin-striped, three-piece suit with appropriate accessories. A white shirt is mandatory. New-line firms, which include many high-tech companies, new manufacturing firms, and assorted other start-up companies that have made it big in the past few years, are generally more casual about dress, although you should check out a company before going on an interview. This means that you need not wear the power suit, but can wear gray or light blue if you want to. You can feel comfortable wearing a light blue shirt or some other neutral color. Your tie must still be conservative, as must be your accessories.

REGIONAL VARIATIONS IN DRESS

As important as industry variations are regional variations in how you dress. On the East Coast and in major urban business centers such as Chicago, Boston, or Atlanta, dress is more conservative. Women and men lean toward conservative business suits.

In the South and the smaller cities of the Midwest, the dress-for-success suit for women has not caught on. Women tend to wear matching outfits and dresses as often as they wear suits. Both men and women wear businesslike clothes, but neither sex pays much attention to the finer points of Malloy's rules. Doubleknits and other synthetic fabrics are worn without apology.

Except for San Francisco and some businesses in Los Angeles, dress tends to be more casual along the West Coast, particularly in Silicon Valley, than in other parts of the country. You can even blow an interview with some high-tech companies by showing up overdressed. A sports jacket and tie are often the rule in some of these companies, where employees take pride in their laid-back corporate culture.

The biggest differences in dress exist between New York City and the rest of the country. If you're from another part of the country, and you're interviewing in Manhattan, it is easy to feel like a hick if you don't understand the dress code.

Business dress is conservative, as you would expect, but there are a few other rules peculiar to New York. Both men and women tend to wear dark colors, probably because the city is dirty and light colors can pick up dirt during one day's wearing. A white suit or pastel suit or outfit would look out of place at any Wall Street firm, even on a scorchingly hot summer day. In some businesses, most notably banking, stockbrokering, and most old-line manufacturing companies, a dress-for-success suit is as imperative for women as a three-piece suit is for men. Men tend to wear white or blue shirts for interviews. A club tie plays better in this part of the country than it does in the Midwest or even on the West Coast, but lapel pins signifying membership in an organization are taboo.

Many New Yorkers are snobs about fabrics and prefer to wear only natural ones. This still doesn't mean a woman should risk wearing a linen dress for an interview, however; if you must, opt for a linen and synthetic blend that won't wrinkle. Polyester and obvious synthetics, however, are frowned on, and an $800 knit suit won't be considered as classy as a $450 suit in wool. Wear natural fiber, dark, conservative clothes, and you'll be set to conquer the Big Apple.

The variations that occur in dress are often as individual to a particular firm as they are to an industry or an area of the country, so, if possible, always check out how you should dress for a specific interview. Ask someone who has already interviewed there. Ask an executive recruiter. When in doubt, always go with a conservative look.

·| ELEVEN |·
Self-Confidence and Anxiety

While a little bit of anxiety may be charming in someone young and inexperienced—the rare new graduate who suffers from it, for example—it is deadly during an executive interview. You must be self-confident.

WHY YOU NEED SELF-CONFIDENCE

Self-confidence is an important part of the first impression you create during an interview. A prospective employer can easily take one look at a job candidate and decide how self-confident—or how anxious—he or she is. It shows in the way you enter a room, the way you carry your coat and briefcase, the way you dress, the way you stand—in short, in just about everything about you. And self-confidence is not something you can fake. It is not so much what you say as how you present yourself.

Self-confidence is absolutely necessary if you are to interview well. It is what lets you go into an interview on a peer basis, according to Millie McCoy: "I think the more confident person, the better executive, goes into an interview knowing that it is a peer relationship. The insecure person is uncomfortable with the relationship."

Self-confidence can backfire on you, though, if you're not careful. Too much self-confidence during an interview may be a sign that your ego needs are high, that you're not really going to be a team player, or even that you're a little too arrogant or snobbish, all reasons that employers frequently cite for not hiring an otherwise qualified and experienced person.

Furthermore, no matter how self-confident you think you are, you also have to convince someone else—the interviewer—that you're on top of things. Something that job candidates don't always remember is that it takes two to create a first impression. You may be so sure you're perceived as powerful and aggressive that you fail to see that you haven't made quite the same impression on the person who is interviewing you. That's why it's important during an interview to watch not only your body language but also the body language of the person who interviews you.

ANXIETY

The opposite of self-confidence is anxiety. Several recruiters said anxiety is the single biggest reason that people fail in executive interviews.

Unfortunately, anxiety sometimes is difficult to control when you are job-hunting. It is even tougher to control when you're under pressure to find a job. If you have been fired and don't have much leverage regarding how long you can go without a job, that's a special problem. Your anxiety level goes up, and this inevitably interferes with the way you present yourself, as well as with the impact you have on interviewers.

Don't confuse anxiety with enthusiasm. Many job candidates

think they can pass off their anxiety as enthusiasm, but emotions don't work that way. Enthusiasm does impress a prospective employer, and in fact you must be enthusiastic to get a job. Anxiety, on the other hand, is deadly, and any interviewer will be able to tell the difference between a kind of of frenetic energy that is anxiety and genuine enthusiasm.

How You Can Develop Self-Confidence and Reduce Anxiety

Within limits you can train yourself to become more self-confident and less anxious. Both are, after all, states of mind.

Raising your self-confidence and reducing your anxiety requires, above all else, a positive state of mind. You have to learn to view yourself in the best possible light and to view your work experience in the same way, or as one executive recruiter put it, "You have to be disciplined. You have to fight against the anxiety, especially if you really need to find a job. You have to realize that whether you are out of a job or not, a mistake in choosing your next job could be disastrous for your career. Even if you are out of a job, you must approach this decision—the entire job-hunting process, for that matter—as if you had a job."

Write Mental Scripts for Yourself

One way to build your self-confidence and reduce your anxiety is to figure out what is making you anxious. Has your present employer basically told you to look for another job even though you are still officially employed? Have you been told that you have a year to look around? Were you fired from your last job? Are you still on the job but have a firing in your past that will make you anxious about job-hunting?

Once you have identified what is causing your anxiety, you can do something about it. Start by dealing separately with each issue that is causing you anxiety. If, for example, you are worried because you were fired, sit down and analyze the reasons that you were fired. Figure out a way to describe them in as positive a light as possible. Decide exactly how you will explain the firing to anyone who interviews you. In other words, write a mental script that will help you cope with the awkward situation. When you have handled one fear, move on to the next one, repeating the process until you have devised positive, logical explanations for each of the problems you expect to encounter when you interview.

Practice Makes Perfect

The next step is to practice, trite as that may sound. Practice in front of a mirror or with a friend. Role play, if necessary. The more you repeat the mental scripts you have written for yourself, the more self-confident you will be when you deliver them "in performance," as it were. Bob Hecht, who believes that the value of practice cannot be stressed too much, noted, "You've got to practice. Behavior rehearsals are very important. The more you practice, the easier it becomes to answer the difficult questions. The easier it becomes to present and smooth out your answers, the more honest and natural your presentation will sound. You simply have to practice answering the questions that will be asked, especially the hard ones such as why you were fired. You have to be well prepared to deal with the hard issues that come up during a job interview."

Maintain the Feeling That You Are in Control

It's important to maintain the feeling that you are in control to some degree during an interview. In part, you can accomplish this by managing the interview and the interviewer in the ways that have been suggested throughout this book. Another way to maintain a feeling of control is to become an astute observer of the interviewer's body language. Here are some suggestions for doing that:

• **An offer of food or cigarettes at the start of an interview is a signal that the interviewer has a casual, friendly attitude.** Although you're better off not taking any food or cigarettes, do take note.

• **When an interviewer leans back in a chair, this means that he or she is ready to listen.** The small talk has ended, and the serious part of the interview has now begun.

• **If the interviewer looks away while you are speaking, don't necessarily take this as a sign that something is wrong or that he or she is bored.** This may be a message that the interviewer is listening and weighing what you are saying. Some inexperienced job candidates read this message correctly but respond to it incorrectly. They think they must keep talking until the interviewer makes direct eye contact with them again. So they ramble on a bit longer than they should. Simply say what you have to say and then stop talking. Wait until the interviewer picks up the thread of the conversation again.

Perhaps this is the place to say something about silences in conversations. Inexperienced interviewers often think they are in control only when they are talking. Nothing could be further from the truth. It's when you talk on and on that you tend to lose control and get into trouble during an interview. The better part of being in control often consists of turning an interview back to the interviewer.

Also important to remember is that silences have many meanings, some of which aren't necessarily bad. A silence can be approving or disapproving. It can mean the listener is contemplating something you have said. It's very important not to panic during a silence and say things you may later regret.

• **When the interviewer nods as you talk, this can generally be taken as a sign of agreement.** But don't forget that some interviewers will also nod sympathetically to encourage you to go on at greater length about something they don't necessarily agree with or may even disapprove of. The overall tone of the interview will also help you to know the difference between a nod that spells agreement and one that may not.

• **When an interviewer lowers his or her voice while talking to you, this is good.** It means that you are being taken into the interviewer's confidence.

• **A cold, blank stare when you say something means that what you said has met with disapproval.** Don't panic when you get this reaction. Change the subject or wrap up what you are saying and wait for the interviewer to make the next move. One small gaffe hardly means that the entire interview is lost.

• **If the interviewer looks at his or her watch or the door, starts to rearrange papers on his desk, or changes positions frequently in his chair, these are signs of impatience.** They may mean you have lost the interviewer's attention, but more likely, if the interview has gone well, such gestures may simply mean that the interview is coming to an end because the interviewer has something else to do.

Paying attention to these body-language messages from the interviewer will increase your sense of being on top of an interview and will make you feel more in control. This, in turn, reduces your anxiety and makes you feel more self-confident.

Watch Your Own Body Language

The final thing you can do to project self-confidence and reduce your anxiety is to be aware of the messages your own body language sends to the interviewer.

Your body language is vitally important during an interview. You can project an image of self-confidence without ever opening your mouth. And you can also betray anxiety without ever saying a word.

Signs that you are a self-confident person include a good, firm handshake, straight posture, a smiling face, sitting comfortably in a chair, and making good eye contact.

A good, firm handshake is one of the first signals you can give someone to show that you're self-confident. An amazing number of people reach adulthood without mastering this simple social maneuver. Some people err by giving a bone-crunching handshake, but that is somehow less offensive than a limp, weak handshake.

The kind of handshake you give during an interview should also never step over the border into a social handshake. Put your hand—your whole hand, not just your fingers—into the other person's hand and grasp his or her hand for a second or two. Don't squeeze, especially if you are shaking the hand of a member of the opposite sex; too much could be read into this.

Don't touch the person with your other hand. This is a small but important point. Except among very good friends meeting socially, touching the other person this way is the prerogative of the person who has the most power, which means the person interviewing you. If you watched the televised 1984 presidential debates, you saw a good example of this. President Ronald Reagan reached out to grasp the arm of Vice-President Walter Mondale when they shook hands at the start of the debates. It would not have been appropriate for Walter Mondale to touch the President of the United States that way. It's similar to the rule that says you don't ever touch the Queen of England.

Good posture is also important. You should not stand ramrod straight, or you will end up looking anxious and ill-at-ease. Just be sure you stand upright as opposed to slouching.

Walk into an interview with a friendly smile on your face. You needn't smile throughout the interview because this is indeed serious business, but that initial smile is important in establishing the fact that you feel good about yourself.

Another thing that announces your self-confidence is the way you sit in a chair during an interview. Slouching does not look casually self-confident; it looks sloppy. Sitting too straight looks anxious. Get settled in the chair when you sit down. Put your outer wraps somewhere else so you aren't shifting them around on your lap during the interview. Put your briefcase beside the chair where you can get it if you need it, but where it isn't in the way.

The last important way to show self-confidence is through eye contact. It's important to look someone in the eye when you first meet him and to maintain steady eye contact through out the interview. Americans, though, aren't given to staring intently at one another, so be careful that you don't overdo the eye contact.

The worst sin, however, is to avoid eye contact. If you do this, you'll look shifty and may leave the person interviewing you with the feeling that you aren't honest.

People sometimes manage to send out signals that they are self-confident, but then they override those signals with ones that announce their insecurity. The clues that you are feeling unusually anxious (everyone is a little bit anxious during anything as important as an interview) can be verbal and nonverbal.

You give away your anxiety verbally when you repeatedly ask if there is anything else you can tell the person interviewing you or if you press him or her to tell you when a decision will be made. It's one thing to press an interviewer for a decision when you clearly have one to make and you're interested if this position (and have reason to believe they are interested in you, too). It's another thing entirely to press because you're experiencing uncontrollable anxiety. Don't ask when a decision will be made and don't pressure to find out when you can call for a decision. Such tactics might work for new graduates, but they should be beneath the dignity of an executive.

Another sign of anxiety is sweaty palms. If this is a problem, try washing your hands in cold water and drying them very thoroughly when you arrive for the interview. If you can't keep your palms from sweating, then ignore them. Don't comment on them and reinforce the initial first impression they give. If you ignore them and otherwise make a good impression, they'll be forgotten soon enough.

Just as you practiced the answers you would give to tough questions you expected to be asked, you can also practice to minimize your anxiety. Ask a friend or spouse to put you through a trial interview. This may not stress you enough to make all your bad traits show up, but whoever helps you will spot some problem areas.

Above all, as you go into an executive interview, keep in mind that you have some special skills and a great deal of experience to sell. If you didn't, you wouldn't have gotten the interview in the first place. Also keep in mind that you wouldn't be going into this interview if you weren't already an executive. People who aren't executives don't get invitations to executive interviews. It's a basic ground rule of interviewing. And most important, keep in mind that the person interviewing you really wants to fill the position (99 percent of the time, anyway), and that he or she will be delighted if you turn out to be the person for the job.

TWELVE

Tough Talk: Negotiating Your Way Into the Job

At some point during the first interview, you'll begin to develop some sense of whether or not you want the job you're interviewing for. If you do, you'll want a second interview. Whether or not you get a second interview depends on how well the first interview goes. If it goes well, the prospective employer will see you as a viable job candidate.

Usually, the first interview is a getting-to-know-you session. If a recruiter has been involved, you may not even discuss the specifics of the job. But, according to most headhunters, if you do get into discussing salary on the first interview, then you know that it has gone very well indeed.

Since few interviewers broach the subject of salary during a first interview, however, how do you tell when a second interview is in the offing? You look for some response on the part of the person interviewing you that he or she is eager to see you again. Comments such as "Well, your qualifications seem to fit our job description" or "You seem to have the kind of experience we've been looking for" are clues that you've passed the first interview with flying colors. Some interviewers will refer to other job candidates and what they were lacking. If what they were lacking is something you have, you can be pretty sure you're becoming a more viable candidate by the minute. Other interviewers will come right out and invite you back for a second interview; they're eager to tell you what the next step is.

On occasion, you can take the initiative in setting up a second interview. If an interviewer has expressed an interest in you, and you, in turn, have expressed an interest in the company, then the logical next question from an interviewee is: "Well, where do we go from here?" To which the answer will nearly always be an invitation for a second interview or a description of the hiring process so you will know what the next step is if it isn't an interview.

Don't ask what the next step is when the interview was set up through an executive recruiter. You should still be playing a little hard to get at the end of the first interview. Let the company woo you; let them think that you aren't so eager to pursue this. In this situation, the initiative for setting up the interview is left entirely up to the company. As a rule, though, you won't have to wait long to find out what's happening. The recruiter will know within a day or so how the interview went, and he'll level with you about it.

You can sometimes set up further interviews, so long as they are not to negotiate the terms of the job. Al Duarte noted that a job candidate who is being wooed into a job is in an especially good position to write his or her own ticket with regard to a second interview, *so long as the purpose of the interview is not to negotiate the terms of the job.* He said, "You can do more than drop hints about certain kinds of interviews. You can say, 'I want to come out and see your plant.' 'I want to meet your financial vice-president.' In effect, you can tell them how you want the interviewing process to go to some extent." Of course, this works only if you have been set up for the interview by a recruiter—and if you know the company is interested in you. The act of opening negotiations, furthermore, is still in the hands of the company. A word of warning: Although a company won't mind your requesting more interviews, they won't necessarily grant them. One major manufacturing firm schedules only two interviews regardless of whether or not the job candidate wants more.

WHO CONDUCTS THE SECOND INTERVIEW?

Generally, a second interview and any other interviews are with line executives rather than with human resources people, although human resources personnel may sit in on some or all of the interviews. In most companies, an offer for an executive job comes from the line executive who will be your immediate superior, but occasionally the offer is formally made through human resources.

THE PURPOSE OF A SECOND INTERVIEW— AND ANY OTHERS

Several things may happen during a second interview. While negotiations are uppermost in everyone's mind, this is hardly the only reason to conduct a second interview.

A second interview provides an opportunity for the interviewer to investigate your background a little more thoroughly. If you're invited back for a second interview for any reason, you have passed muster in the important areas of personality and matching the corporate culture. People occasionally go back to second (and even third, fourth, and fifth) interviews and don't get hired, but no one ever gets invited back for a second interview unless he will fit in with the culture.

In the first interview, the people you talked to have gotten to know you, but there may remain several areas they would like to probe more thoroughly. You may be asked to explain certain aspects of your past experience or qualifications in greater detail.

A second interview may be scheduled for purposes of psychological testing and job simulation. Psychological testing, as noted earlier, has made a comeback after several years of being out of favor as an interviewing technique. Al Duarte described the situation these days, saying, "Most companies use testing not as the deciding factor, but as one of many tools. Generally, if it's a company policy that you must take tests, then you must do it if you want to work for the company. Only at the very top levels—the top two people, for example—is the testing sometimes not done." But even being interviewed for a CEO position doesn't necessarily exempt you from testing these days. William Byham noted the trend toward extending both simulation and psychological testing to "extremely high levels—including CEOs and division managers."

The most important reason for a second interview is to negotiate the terms of the job. You should go into any second interview well aware that this may be on the agenda. And you need to be prepared for some tough talk.

Being in the right frame of mind helps. Acknowledge to yourself the importance of these negotiations and prepare yourself to take an aggressive stance. But even though you should feel some control over the situation, you should also acknowledge that the company has control, too—and also some preset limits.

Think of job negotiations in the same way that you would think of any other business deal because you have just as much—and perhaps more—to gain or lose in these negotiations. Just because you both like each other and want to form a partnership doesn't mean the negotiations won't be tough. They should be—and they almost invariably are.

Prepare a wants list that you'll use to negotiate your terms. You should always go into a second interview with a mental wants list. Stay flexible, but keep in mind a compensation range that will be acceptable to you, as well as a clear outline of the perks you're seeking.

Finally, keep in mind that no two negotiating situations are ever alike. However much you prepare for the second interview, this is one time when you'll also have to think on your feet.

THE ONLY THEORY OF NEGOTIATION YOU'LL EVER NEED TO KNOW

Most managers are quite adept at negotiations, or they wouldn't already be managers. And if you do need to brush up on your negotiating skills (not a bad idea before taking on a major, important interview that could change your life), there are some excellent books in this area, among them *Salary Strategies*, by Marilyn Moats Kennedy (Bantam, 1983); *Getting to Yes*, by Roger Fisher and William Ury (Penguin, 1983); and *Winning By Negotiation*, by Tessa Albert Warschaw (McGraw-Hill, 1980).

As you embark on negotiations of any kind, it's important to understand one basic principle: Negotiation is all about giving and taking. Even if you normally play hardball and will do almost anything to win, you still may have to give up something in order to get something. In job negotiations there are two levels of giving up: permanent and deferred.

You may have to give up something permanently because the interviewer flatly refuses to give it to you. For example, you may ask for a company-paid vacation only to be told it's out of the question. Score a loss. A permanent loss. There is no way you can get that particular perk.

Then there are the things that you defer because in doing so you can get them later. You want a guaranteed bonus; the company wants to see how you perform before they commit to that. You settle by saying you'll take the bonus after six months when they review your work. They agree. That's a deferred benefit. It's good. Score one for you.

Even the largest, most policy-oriented company will strike individual deals. When you're dealing with the human resources department, the official line is often that they can't give you something because they haven't given it to anyone else. Keep pushing a while longer, especially with whoever will be your boss. As one management consultant noted: "The man at the top gets what he wants." Besides, all rules are made to have exceptions. One of your goals in negotiating should be to be one of the exceptions.

Once negotiations start, there are two broad areas to cover: salary and perks. Usually discussion opens with talk of salary. But it may or may not be firmed up before you move onto the subject of perks. It's a good negotiating tactic to settle one issue at a time, but if you can't settle salary to your satisfaction, move on to perks with the idea that you'll return to the topic of salary—and also with the idea that if you get some good perks, you'll be more inclined to settle on the issue of salary.

Talking Salary
Who Opens Negotiations?

The interviewer always opens the negotiations about salary. He or she will usually broach the subject by asking what kind of compensation package you are looking for. Sometimes, he will even dispense with the euphemistic conversation and ask you directly what you need to earn to take this job.

Know What the Going Rate Is

Executive salaries, like other items in a company's budget, are subject to the vagaries of the economy. When the economy is booming, employers are more generous in what they pay; when the economy is not doing well, they are stingier. The range of increase is wide and varies depending upon the industry you're in, but generally you can expect a raise of anywhere from 5 to 25 percent of your present salary. But remember that an executive salary is only part of a total compensation package, and it's a surprisingly small part at that. In a typical executive compensation package, the salary accounts for 48 percent of the total; bonuses, for 17 percent; health and other fringe benefits, for 14 percent; stock options and other long-term incentives, for 20 percent, and luxury perks, for 1 percent.*

Furthermore, if you're at or near the top of the salary scale for your field, you'll have to decide whether to accept a lateral move, or whether some additional compensation apart from salary will be necessary to woo you away from your present employer. This is why having a good idea of the benefits you want is so important.

Executive and middle-management salaries, as one might suppose, also vary with the geographic location of the company. Salaries are highest in New York City, followed by the Southwest, Chicago, and California. According to statistics published by Hay Associates, an executive in New York City typically earns $151,000, and the average middle-management salary is around $59,000. In the Southwest (Dallas and the Baton Rouge area), the next-highest-paid region, a top executive earns about $116,000, and a middle manager earns about $52,000. The lowest salaries are paid in the Midwest (Chicago excluded), the South, and the West, excluding California.

---

* *U.S. News & World Report*, "What Executives Are Getting Paid," October 17, 1983, page 72.

Can You Pad Your Present Salary?

In the words of Janet Tweed, "Lying doesn't work for executives." She does, however, suggest a way that you can explain your salary needs: "Let's say you're working for $42,000 a year, and you're being interviewed for a $58,000-a-year job. You say you're only interested in the position at $60,000. The employer will tell you no, that he'll never give you a $20,000-a-year raise. But if you can justify that raise, you're liable to get it. If, for example, you can say that your company had a salary freeze for two years, or that another company is, in fact, interested in hiring you for $60,000, or that you're moving from Mississippi to New York City, then you've explained why you need $60,000. You should try to do this without stating your present salary or lying about it." She added, "I think it's fair to say that another company is interested in you. You can also say that you're presently interviewing in the range of $62,000 to $85,000. Let's say you're interviewing with a company that wants to pay you $70,000 to $72,000. When they hear your range, they may reach to their top dollar and hope you don't take a job on money alone."

Applying Pressure

The time when you discuss salary is also the best time to apply any pressure needed to hasten the negotiations along their way. One job candidate said she learned how to apply this kind of pressure after a few interviews. When asked about salary, she often responded, "I've got a company I like a lot that's only offering $50,000, but there's another company that's offering $62,000. I'm presently talking to three companies. I'm on my second interview with both of them. To be honest with you, I like your situation very much. I'm telling you this so I don't lose the opportunity of being considered further by having to make up my mind." Several executive recruiters said this kind of pressure almost always works if you dish it out honestly and keep things nice and straight.

If a company is interested in you, they won't be put off by the fact that they have some competition. If anything, this will pique their interest, spur them to make a speedier offer than they might otherwise have made, and possibly improve the deal you are able to strike with them, if not always in terms of salary, then certainly in terms of benefits.

TALKING PERKS

Before you enter into any negotiations, you need to know what you want to get out of them, particularly with regard to perks. After a certain point, most executives are better off taking a smaller income increase than they might otherwise and letting their prospective employers sweeten their compensation package with all kinds of goodies in the form of perks. After all, Uncle Sam only eats up the extra income. Another reason it's important to know what perks you want before you begin to negotiate is that different kinds of perks do different things for you.

Kinds of Perks

Some perks let you pass along some of your personal expenses to your employer. Examples of this kind of perk are relocation expenses, insurance, parking expenses, tax-return preparation, and financial counseling. Some newer perks include such things as home computers, home burglar alarms, and even home WATS lines. Many companies pick up the tab for education bills, either for college or for special education.

Another category of perks provides status. These include first-class air travel, expense accounts, certain kinds of cars, chauffeurs in some cases, and club dues and related expenses.

Status perks have fallen into disuse in recent years, mostly because executives have begun to realize how little they have to show for such perks after they leave a company. These are also the perks the IRS is most likely to question, and they are likely to be lost in any major tax reform. In some corporate cultures, status perks are frowned upon because they set executives apart from other workers. In a culture where teamwork is highly valued, for example, giving country-club memberships to the five top employees isn't the way to encourage it.

The last category of perks includes those that provide long-term security. These days, the most typical perks in this category are equity and incentive programs.

Large, publicly held firms are more likely than small, and often, privately held firms to part with equity. Even if you get equity from a smaller firm, be sure that it also entitles you to a voice in management. Owning stock in a small, privately held firm isn't worth much if you don't have a say in how the company is run.

Privately held companies often provide stock to executives through what are called phantom stock arrangements. With phantom stock, an executive comes into the company knowing that he can't gain any kind of voting shares but that shares will be put aside for him. He can cash them on a deferred compensation basis, which usually means at retirement or at the end of a specified period of time such as five years.

In some companies, salaries and bonuses are tied to incentive programs. (About half of all companies still give bonuses on a purely discretionary basis, but this practice is losing out to incentive-based bonuses.) Bonuses are frequently tied to sales performances, marketing performance, and profit goals.

Raises are sometimes tied to incentive programs these days, and you may find that you come out ahead negotiating your raises on this basis. Any kind of incentive programs can stand to increase your earnings significantly. Needless to say, the time to negotiate these matters is when you take the job.

Other Things You Need to Know to Negotiate Perks

Perks shift with the times. For example, bonuses fall off during a recession. When the economy picks up, they come back, to quote one executive recruiter, bigger and more beautiful than ever before.

Interest rates are another example of a perk that changes with the times. When interest rates are high, mortgage differentials are an important perk. When interest rates fall, this perk becomes less important.

The newest category of perks includes what might be called spouse perks. When one partner in a two-career couple takes a job that involves relocation, a company can provide one of several perks for the spouse who must also relocate. It can help the spouse find another job, offer a relocation allowance, and, in some instances, even hire the spouse. The latter is not so outlandish as it may seem at first reading. People often marry people who work in the same field they do, and even some old-line manufacturing firms have no objection to spouses working for the company provided they don't work in the same department.

Contracts are another important executive perk. Any contract must be negotiated carefully. It's legitimate to ask at an early stage of negotiations—or even early on during the interview process—whether or not a contract is available. An executive recruiter always knows whether or not one is being offered.

Contracts favor executives and offer additional security. The only time they don't favor the executive is when they contain a noncompete clause. If there is a noncompete clause, you'll have to decide whether the benefits of the contract outweigh the possibility that you might not be free to look for another job in the same industry.

The most important element of a contract is the severance pay arrangement. In these days of mercurial management when no one is exempt from a sudden and often erratically inspired firing, it's just common sense to have a contract that provides for a hefty severance. Most contracts guarantee salary for six months to a year.

Who gets contracts these days? CEOs invariably get them if they want them, at least in large, publicly held corporations. Division managers are frequently entitled to contracts, and sometimes even middle managers negotiate them. More typically, though, middle managers get—and should ask for—a letter of intent.

A letter of intent should spell out the perks you have negotiated, and, more important, any perks that have been promised at a future date. For example, suppose that you are hired in as a vice-president with the promise that you will become a senior vice-president at the next board meeting. That's the kind of thing that should be outlined in a letter of intent or a contract.

Another category of perks worth mentioning are those you get when you relocate overseas. Executive recruiters say they're always generous. One noted, "Overseas compensation is a whole different ball game when you are talking perks. Overseas housing allowances, living allowances, education allowances, and travel allowances are all standard."

Who Negotiates Perks?

Unlike salary, a subject that is always introduced by the interviewer, perks are often brought up by the interviewee. Never be shy about asking for what you want in the way of perks, and keep in mind that they are the most negotiable items in a compensation package. Sometimes you'll get a flat no, but more often, if you aren't given a perk you ask for outright, a deal will be worked out whereby you get it at a later date, or you'll be offered something else in place of the perk you requested.

Having a reason that you need a perk may help. Keep the reasons businesslike and honest. The very best way to get a perk is to say that you have it (if you do with your present employer). No one wants to have something taken away, so your prospective employer will be inclined to give you the perks you presently have and then to throw in a few more to make the package look more attractive to you

Don't use personal reasons to explain why you need a particular perk. For example, you should ask for a salary differential if you are going to relocate to a part of the country that is particularly expensive, but you shouldn't say that your family can barely make ends meet at the present time and you know you'll need a lot more money to live in the new city.

Of course, you will only want some perks for highly personal reasons, and these will have to be dealt with directly. If for example, your spouse will need some help in relocating, then that is a personal need that you'll have to discuss directly. If you want an educational perk for a child who requires special education, that, too, is the kind of thing you'll need to discuss in personal terms. What you don't do is state or even hint that you need a particular salary or perk because you're barely getting by on what you now make or because you have alimony to pay or some other highly personal expense.

When you use personal excuses as reasons that you need a particular salary or perk, you denigrate your skills. You wouldn't ask a boss for a raise after you had been on a job for a while and tell him you need it because you want to buy a new car. You would argue that you want a raise because you had been a productive worker and you deserve it. Be sure you use the same kind of solid reasoning when you are negotiating to take a job.

ACCEPTING A JOB

Once salary and perks have been negotiated, you are ready to accept the job formally. The job was offered at the start of negotiations, and acceptance comes when everyone has agreed to the salary and benefits package.

There are two theories of how an executive should accept a job when it is offered to him or her.

Some experts say a job should be accepted on the spot. Not to accept immediately is to look indecisive, which is bad enough for a manager, or worse, if you delay, you may look as if you've got another job dangling.

Other experts say a job should never be accepted on the spot. Doing so makes you look impulsive. Delaying acceptance makes you look measured and mature in your judgments.

The truth, of course, is somewhere in the middle. You don't have to accept on the spot because in the words of one recruiter, "A decision as important as this is at least worth a walk around the block." On the other hand, you can't afford to play games at this stage of the interview process.

Bob Maddocks at RCA said he would find unnecessary delays disconcerting in a case where his company was ready to hire: "Some people may need to talk to their family, and that may take a while. I would hope that the person has already done this before the interview. If the interviewing process has really gone well, and we're clear about wanting someone, and that person has been clear about what he or she wants, then if someone says he has to think about a job when we offer it to him, something is wrong."

Lots of employers and executive recruiters stressed that the time to discuss a potential job with one's family is before the interview process begins. It's okay to check back with the family one last time before taking a job, but it's not okay to use the family as a reason that you need several days to think about an offer that you have already negotiated.

DECLINING GRACIOUSLY

Sometimes the problem is not how to accept a job, but, rather, how to decline one. It's not unusual for a highly qualified manager who has waged a full-scale job search to find himself or herself with two or three offers. At such fortuitous moments, you may find yourself declining one job at the same time you accept another. The only guideline for declining a job offer is to do it graciously. *Never* burn bridges you want want to cross again some day.

IN CONCLUSION

Interviewing is the most challenging experience in the job-hunting process. The most highly skilled job hunter usually can use some assistance in this area. But interviewing also is—and will always remain—a highly individual process. No two interviewers are alike. No two interviewees are alike. And certainly, no two interviews ever progress in the same way.

Furthermore, an interview is one of those life situations where you must think on your feet. All the preparation in the world won't make up for an inability to handle each situation as it comes along. Because of this, the very best way to handle each and every interview is to follow what you have learned in these pages and then trust your instincts. That and a little bit of luck will get you through every time with flying colors.

Index